Realm
of the
Rising Sun

Realm
of the
Rising Sun

JAPANESE MYTH

METRO BOOKS
NEW YORK

MYTH AND MANKIND

REALM OF THE RISING SUN: Japanese Myth

Writers: Tony Allan (Japan: A Land Apart, The Legacy of Japanese Myth),
Michael Kerrigan (A Nation of Heroes, Supernatural Forces),
Charles Phillips (A Universe of Gods, The Divine Dynasty)
Consultant: C. Scott Littleton

Created, edited and designed by
Duncan Baird Publishers
Castle House
75–76 Wells Street
London W1P 3RE

Duncan Baird Publishers
Managing Editor: Diana Loxley
Managing Art Editor: Clare Thorpe
Series Editor: Christopher Westhorp
Editor: Christopher Westhorp
Designer: Christine Keilty
Picture Researchers: Cecilia Weston-Baker
Commissioned Illustrations: Neil Gower
Map Artwork: Lorraine Harrison
Artwork Borders: Iona McGlashan
Editorial Researcher: Clifford Bishop

Staff for *Realm of the Rising Sun: Japanese Myth*
Editorial Manager: Tony Allan
Design Consultant: Mary Staples
Editorial Production: Ruth Vos

Metro Books
122 Fifth Avenue
New York, NY 10011

ISBN-13: 978-1-4351-0607-9
ISBN-10: 1-4351-0607-5

Printed and bound in China

10 9 8 7 6 5 4 3 2 1

Title page: A mother and daughter viewing fireflies. In Japan, these glowing beetles are said to be the souls of the dead, and gathering of them might indicate the scene of battle long ago. Firefly Catching by Eishosai Choki, c.1794-95.

Contents page: Ivory carving of an elderly woodsman pouring himself a fortifying cup of sake rice wine; late 19th century.

Contents

JAPAN: A LAND APART

Mr Matsui does not exist, but millions like him do in modern Japan. He is, let's say, a salaryman in an electronics conglomerate, working long hours at the office each day before commuting back to his home and family in a distant Tokyo suburb. In many ways his life is very much like that of office-workers in London or Lisbon, Sao Paulo or Seattle.

But there is one marked difference. Being of conservative temperament, he likes to pause for a few minutes each day in a small shrine on the roof of the building where he works. It is dedicated to Inari, once a local rice god but now venerated as a patron of prosperity. And occasionally he packs his wife and children into the family Toyota to drive 500 kilometres to Ise to pay homage at the grand shrine of Amaterasu, the sun goddess who almost 3,000 years ago – according to Shinto tradition – sent her grandson down to Earth to be Japan's first ruler.

The survival of Shinto beliefs in technologically advanced Japan is one of the odder phenomena of world mythology, almost as if Greeks were still to worship Zeus and Hera or Swedes to reverence Odin. In part they owe their longevity to political factors, for from early times the country's rulers have periodically used them to bolster the authority of the state. As important or more, though, is the way in which they are meshed into the very fabric of Japan: into the physical landscape as well as the mental hinterland of traditions.

For Shinto – literally "The Way of the Gods" – has its roots in ancient nature worship. Its first deities were the spirits that resided in mountains and waterfalls, in eroded sea-cliffs or sacred groves of trees. In time human interpreters would impose order on this formless world. They gave the faith a royal family of gods parallelling the imperial dynasty on Earth, and even linked the two in a single line of descent.

Yet even now, when the emperors have renounced their claim to divinity, the gods have kept a place in Japanese affections. Partly they have survived because the stories about them are memorable, populated by a cast of characters as passionate in their quarrels and reconciliations as Greece's Olympians. But they also draw from their local roots a continuity that entwines them inextricably into the nation's oldest traditions. For Mr Matsui and many like him, Japan would not be Japan without its myths.

Above: A 17th-century Buddhist reliquary or *sharito* in the form of a bronze pagoda.

Opposite: One of the best-known symbols of Japan, the red Akino Miyajima Great Torii rising out of the sea, as seen from the window of Itsukushima Shrine, Miyajima Island. The shrine is dedicated to the divine daughters of the storm god Susano.

7

The Japanese People

The sea has always set Japan apart. The strait separating the island nation from the mainland is 190 kilometres wide even at its narrowest point opposite Korea's southern tip. As for China, it is, even at its closest, all of 725 kilometres away across a perilous channel.

The sea's waters have also divided the Japanese from one another, cutting up their homeland into four main islands and literally thousands of smaller ones. The giants – Kyushu in the south and Hokkaido in the north, with Honshu and Shikoku forming the middle – are themselves intersected by mountain ranges that cover almost 80 per cent of the land area. In this forbidding but beautiful country, the bulk of the populace has always been squeezed into a few rich alluvial valleys and plains, the largest of them in southeastern Honshu around present-day Tokyo, Kyoto and Nagoya. Even now this region is home to almost half the country's population.

From the start, Japan was also a violent land. Three of the great tectonic plates that make up the Earth's crust meet beneath it, frequently grinding together to generate sometimes catastrophic seismic shocks. One-tenth of the world's active volcanoes are here, and earthquakes are a regular occurrence, with more than 1,000 perceptible tremors every year. Undersea eruptions give rise to the massive and lethal form of tidal wave known as a *tsunami*, while savage typhoons frequently strike in late summer and autumn along Honshu's populous coasts. Small wonder, then, that the inhabitants of such a disaster-prone land should have believed in gods with angry and unpredictable moods.

A food-storage jar adorned with the Jomon culture's distinctive corded patterning, *c*.3000–2000BC.

There have always, of course, been compensations for the region's geophysics. The mountain ranges may have made communications difficult, but they have also helped create a ravishingly beautiful landscape of misty peaks and fast-flowing torrents that has inspired generations of artists and poets. And even though cultivable land is in short supply, making up just 16 per cent of the total area, a generally mild climate and abundant rain make it highly productive, particularly for rice-growing. Even today, the islands are largely self-supporting.

The First Settlers

The origins of the Japanese people melt backwards into the mists of time. Until the ending of the last Ice Age, land-bridges connected the islands to Korea and to Siberia, turning the Sea of Japan into a gigantic lake. It is possible that the first settlers arrived by foot at this time, possibly some 30,000 years ago.

The archaeological record starts with implements of roughly chipped stone dating back more than 10,000 years. The Palaeolithic groups who made them were supplanted sometime about 8000BC by an altogether more creative group: the people of the Jomon culture, so-called from their cord-marked (*jomon*) pottery incised with patterns made by pressing twisted fibres into the wet clay. This elegant ware has been described as the finest produced by any Stone Age community. Its makers otherwise lived harsh lives, hunting game, gathering nuts, berries and other wild plants, and by fishing. Other arrivals around this time were the Ainu or Yemeshi, Caucasoids whose descendants still survive in Hokkaido to this day (see box, page 11). Some scholars even believe the Ainu to be descendants of the Jomon culture.

Little in the material remains left by these early arrivals gives any hint of where they originally came from. Better clues can be found in the nation's primeval religious traditions, which seem to reflect shamanistic beliefs and practices otherwise familiar from Siberia.

Rice cultivation seems to have reached the islands with yet another group, the Yayoi, who may have been related in some way to pre-Vietnamese Austronesians and distant kin of the Khmer; yet other strands suggest an Indonesian or even Polynesian influence. They arrived first in the part of Kyushu closest to the Korean peninsula, bringing with them paddy-field techniques pioneered in southern China at least two-and-a-half millennia earlier. They also had knowledge of weaving and of metalworking, introducing both bronze and iron concurrently to the islands; in Japan there was no separate Bronze Age.

In time the Yayoi spread out across Kyushu to Honshu, reaching the Tokyo area around the beginning of the Western Christian era. Japan altered greatly during the Yayoi's ascendancy, changing from a nation of hunter-gatherers and slash-and-burn cultivators into one of settled agricultural communities, divided up by its fractured geography into separate, warring clans under increasingly powerful rulers.

In these early centuries, some at least of these groups established political and trading links with the mainland. At a time when Japan itself remained illiterate, Chinese emissaries put down their impressions of the country in writing, and

their reports cast a fascinating light on conditions prevailing there in the mid-third century when they made their visits. They speak of thirty separate kingdoms, all well-ordered and with regular, supervised markets. Taxes were levied and class distinctions maintained. The men were considered law-abiding although with a tendency to drunkenness, the wives faithful and uncomplaining.

Each separate fief had its own ruler, but all were said to recognize the supreme authority of a Yayoi queen the chroniclers named as Pimiko, an archaic form of the modern word *himeko* or

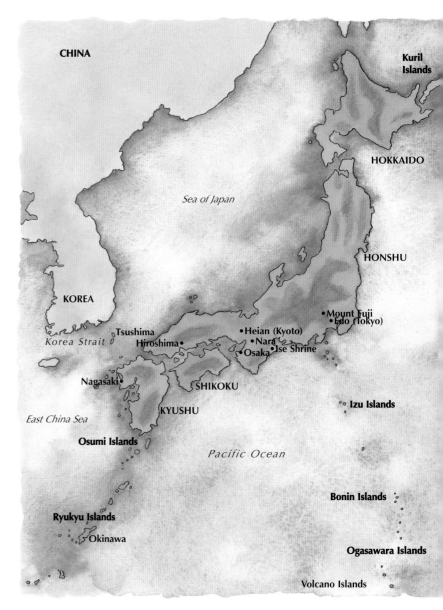

The archipelago of Japan comprises more than 1,000 islands, although most of the land area is made up of just four main ones. Korea's proximity has long been a culturally influential factor.

"princess". Remaining unmarried, this woman lived secluded in a heavily guarded palace, serving deities who rewarded her with the power to foresee the future and bewitch people. A male associate acted as her intermediary, transmitting her wishes to the outside world. When she died she was buried under a great mound, and more than 100 attendants were said to have "followed her to the grave", presumably as sacrificial victims.

In fact the period from about AD300 is known to historians as the Kofun or Burial Mound era, from the distinctive tombs created at the time, many of which had a characteristic keyhole shape. The largest were grandiose in their dimensions. One, traditionally said to be that of the otherwise-unknown Emperor Nintoku, covered thirty-nine hectares surrounded by three separate moats.

Early Religion

The Pimiko story and other evidence provide tantalizing hints of the religious beliefs of these early Japanese. Later sources speak of another powerful woman, the empress Jingo (see page 87), who used rituals to contact deities who then issued advice and warnings through her mouth; in her case, according to the legends, they recommended a successful invasion of Korea. Then there are the small clay figures called *miko* (a word used today for Shinto shrine virgins) found in the fifth-century tumuli; they represent women wearing strange, flattened headgear, possibly prophetesses.

Was there a cult of women of power, who through divine possession had favoured access to the gods? If so, it had disappeared entirely by the time the Japanese historical record opened. Yet some traces may remain. Amaterasu, the principal goddess of the Shinto pantheon, is after all a woman. And even today in Japan there is a countryside tradition of wandering female mediums who are consulted as fortune-tellers; perhaps they are the humble descendants of prophetess-queens.

What is certain is that the foundation upon which all Japan's subsequent beliefs developed was one of shamanism – the belief that certain individuals could, by going into trances, enter the spirit world. The entities they contacted were known as *kami* – deified forces of nature, whether mountains, rivers, oddly shaped rocks, ancient trees or even dead human heroes. The *kami* were not thought of as good or bad but simply as powerful; they needed to be propitiated if they were to look benignly on the people who had dealings with them.

Even in those early times, the individuals who enjoyed privileged access to them were not always women. The Chinese chronicles also speak of diviners who burned bones to determine the future. In particular, they mentioned an

The vast burial tumulus of Emperor Nintoku in the city of Osaka, a 5th-century construction covering an area of 39 hectares, equivalent to the size of three dozen soccer pitches. The enormous mounds were probably introduced to Japan by horse-riding nomads who had originated in Central Asia.

An Indigenous Link with the Past

The Ainu or Yemeshi are the last survivors of the pre-Japanese population of Japan. Driven northwards over the centuries, a few thousand remain on Hokkaido to this day.

Two Ainu men in Hokkaido alongside a bear altar. A bear's spirit was believed to carry messages to the Ainu ancestors.

Nobody knows for sure where the Ainu originally came from, though they are thought to have links with some Caucasoid Siberian peoples. The date of their arrival in Japan is equally a mystery, but archaeological evidence suggests that they have been there for some 5,000 years.

In the past they inhabited all four major islands. Originally hunters, fishermen and trappers, they have always been physically very different from the Japanese; typically they had round eyes and brown hair, and some of the men traditionally sported full beards. Their religion centred on shamanism, and its most important ritual involved the sacrifice of a bear.

By the seventh century AD or earlier, they came into conflict with the Japanese. At first they put up a successful resistance, but were finally overcome in a series of bloody battles at the close of the eighth century.

Thereafter they were gradually driven northwards up to Hokkaido, their final refuge. There they maintained their traditional way of life until comparatively recent times, when it became state policy to assimilate them; they were made to take Japanese names and learn the Japanese language and were encouraged to adopt a settled life as farmers. As a consequence, there are few pure-blooded Ainu left and their language has almost fallen into disuse, despite vigorous attempts by Ainu-rights activists in recent years to preserve it.

individual known as the "keeper of mourning", who was expected to live a life of ascetic self-denial on behalf of the community. "He is not permitted to comb his hair, wash, eat meat or come in contact with women," one envoy reported. "When the people enjoy good fortune, they give him valuable presents; but if they become ill or fare badly, they set it down to his failure to observe his vows, and jointly they put him to death."

Although such figures, like the prophetess queens, had disappeared before Japanese records began, traces of these practices have survived into modern times. There are still ascetics who practice austerities to attain spiritual power, abstaining from eating meat, immersing themselves in ice-cold water and constantly repeating sacred words. Nowadays, though, the recited texts are usually Buddhist, and the whole tradition is strongly influenced by the doctrines of esoteric Buddhism.

The Gift of Literacy

Literacy arrived in Japan from China, and with it came Chinese characters as a medium for writing down the Japanese language.

In AD391, Japanese forces intervened on the Korean peninsula in support of a local ruler. As a gesture of gratitude, he sent a delegation across the Sea of Japan bearing gifts that included a Chinese copybook, *The Thousand Character Classic*. Intrigued, the Japanese court asked him also to dispatch a scholar to teach one of the royal princes to read.

The arrival of this man, the scribe Wani, in the year 405 marked the official adoption of Chinese script by the Japanese. But the marriage of the two wholly dissimilar languages was never an easy one; the tongues have no common ground. The linguistic roots of Japanese are unknown; the use of long, complex sentence structures suggest a Korean mainland link, but the vocabulary dispels it.

Four centuries were to go by before the Japanese found a way of adapting Chinese characters to suit their own special needs. Then, in the ninth century, they adopted the *kana* system by which the complex Chinese ideograms were made to serve simply as phonetic symbols, each corresponding to a syllable in the Japanese tongue.

Thereafter reading and writing became much easier, and literacy spread widely through the samurai warrior class as well as among monks and the nobility. Even so, it was still not unknown, even in medieval times, for scholars to apologize for using Japanese rather than Chinese for fear that it would be incomprehensible to the readers.

Writing styles and uses have varied greatly throughout Japan's history. This woodblock by Utagawa Kunisada, early 19th century, shows a calligraphy party at the Manpachiro teahouse.

The Shinto Pantheon

As for the myths that accompanied the old beliefs, the most important found their way into Shinto, Japan's indigenous religion. Literally "The Way of the Gods", it was in its original form simply a portmanteau for the worship of the *kami*, and as such had neither founder nor sacred book and preached no moral precepts or set doctrine. Its texts spoke of the "800 myriads of gods", shorthand for an innumerable number, for there were more *kami* than anyone could ever hope to count. Shrines were built as dwelling-places for individual divinities, who were propitiated by offerings and prayers. The *kami* were thought to be particularly offended by any contact, even at second- or third-hand, with disease or death, so anyone who had recently been in contact with the sick or dying had to keep well away from all holy places.

In time Shinto took on a slightly more structured shape, emphasizing the primacy of a particular family of gods. The shaping force in this evolution seems to have been political. One of the many clans or *uji* competing for influence in the islands gradually came to establish its pre-eminence. This was the group controlling the fertile Yamato plain on Honshu, where the present-day city of Osaka now stands. They had found their way there from Kyushu, bringing with them the cult of their own tribal divinity Amaterasu, the sun goddess. Their leader ruled in her name, first as a high priest and then as emperor. Extraordinarily enough, the dynasty thus founded so long ago continues to rule Japan to this day.

Over time, the Yamato dynasty shaped the formless mass of Shintoism to suit its own ends. Amaterasu was established as the greatest of the gods, and her shrine at Ise on the Shima peninsula in central Honshu Prefecture, supposedly founded by an emperor's daughter in the first century AD, became Japan's holiest place. The imperial family traced its lineage back to the goddess through a legendary First Emperor, Jimmu Tenno ("Divine Warrior"), traditionally said to have ascended the throne in 660BC, having led the imperial clan from Kyushu to its ultimate home on the Yamato plain.

Ise Jingu, the most sacred shrine complex in Japan, is dedicated to the deity of rice in its outer shrine and the sun goddess in the inner one. The emperor pays an annual visit. These worshippers are depicted in an 18th-century woodblock print.

Over the ensuing centuries, the link was to serve both parties well. While the heavenly connection established the imperial family's divine right to rule, it also ensured the dynasty's unwavering support for the Shinto faith, making the observance of its rites a patriotic duty for all Japanese even when other faiths competed for their spiritual allegiance. The marks of the association were three symbols of majesty – a bronze mirror, a sword and a jewelled fertility necklace (*magatama*) – said to have been presented by Amaterasu to her grandson when she sent him to Earth to rule Japan; they or their successors remain the regalia of the emperor to the present day.

13

An Ordered Society

Japanese society in the late stages of prehistory seems to have been rigidly stratified. The bulk of the population lived in small villages of thatched wooden or bamboo huts, raised off the ground to keep out the damp. They went about barefoot and earned their living in the fields. Their staple food was rice, though other grains were also grown; fish were the main source of protein.

Over the peasantry ruled a land-owning warrior aristocracy who expected to be treated with respect; when a commoner met a noble-man on the road, he had to step aside and squat on his heels or else get down on all fours as a mark of deference. Historians still argue over whether this new ruling class had developed locally or, as might appear more likely, had come to the islands from abroad, possibly Altaic-speakers from Central Asia. They were evidently formidable fighters, riding into battle like medieval European knights on richly caparisoned chargers equipped with saddles and stirrups. Their chosen weapons were longbows and iron swords. These were the men who were buried in the keyhole tombs, and this warrior elite ultimately developed into the samurai class.

As central power spread in Japan, the nation's military and diplomatic ambitions grew. Military expeditions were sent to Korea; Japanese forces may even for a time in the sixth century have exerted control over one of the three kingdoms the peninsula was then divided into.

Yet Korea's great contribution to Japan's development was to be a peaceful one, for it was through that country that the Japanese were exposed to Chinese civilization. The first fruits came as early as AD391, when the ruler of one of the Korean kingdoms showed his grati-tude to Japanese allies who had fought alongside

Koka suit of armour, Edo period 1844–47, devised so as to ease movement while providing protection. Complementing the large cuirass is the sectioned skirt or *kusazuri*, the armoured sleeves or *kote* and the star helmet or *hoshi kabuto,* with neck guard.

The Great Histories

The principal sources for Japanese myth are two early chronicles drawn up by order of the imperial court. The Kojiki *and the* Nihongi *stand at the root of Japanese historical and mythological knowledge. Both works were written at imperial behest in the early years of the eighth century AD.*

The *Kojiki*, or "Record of Ancient Matters", was compiled in AD712 by a scholar named Ono Yasumaro who had been commissioned the previous year by Empress Gemmei. Yasumaro worked from the words of a certain Hiyeda no Are, thought to have been a professional reciter employed to describe great events of history and legend at court on state occasions. Written in a curious mixture of Chinese and Japanese, the *Kojiki* starts in the deep mythological past with the beginning of the world and ends in comparatively recent times with the death of Emperor Suiko in AD641.

Completed eight years later in AD720, the *Nihongi* or *Nihonshoki* – "Chronicles of Japan" – was the work of several scholars writing in classical Chinese and strongly influenced by Chinese and Korean traditions. Intended as a national history of Japan, it was in fact a compilation of myths, legends and poetry as well as an assortment of factual material, running from early times through to the end of the seventh century. Among other innovations, it was the first work to use the term Shinto – "The Way of the Gods" – to describe the nation's distinctive religious traditions.

Both works were initially commissioned by the same empress, and they had an ideological purpose to serve; they consciously sought to shape the nation's most ancient traditions in such a way as to emphasize the central, unquestioned role of the imperial house. In subsequent centuries their importance was inestimable, for they not only helped cement the position of the emperor at the heart of Japanese society but also acted as the vessels in which the Japanese nation's earliest myths were handed down to posterity.

him in a local war by sending a gift of books; with them went scholars who could interpret them, so introducing literacy to the island nation (see box, page 12). Although for some centuries only a tiny minority of people could read, they nonetheless provided a conduit through which the thought of great philosophers such as Confucius and Laozi, the founder of Daoism, could enter the country.

Although Confucianism was to have a profound long-term influence, the Daoist traditions were in many ways closer to Japan's own. In particular, the Daoists' concern with divination meshed with the native prophetic tradition. In time, the Bureau of Divination was to become a prestigious department of Japan's imperial government, charged with the task of examining all policy initiatives in terms of yin and yang, the complementary dualities of traditional Chinese thought; only those that showed a suitable balance between the two were approved. The art of feng shui – Daoist geomancy – was also studied closely; when a new capital was later built at Nara on the Yamato plain, its site was chosen only after lengthy consultation with experts in the subject, and the layout was modelled on that of the chief city of China's Tang dynasty, Changan.

The Coming of Buddhism

Inevitably the imported ideas aroused hostility among some sections of the warrior aristocracy, who reckoned they had more to gain from the preservation of the status quo. But the cause of change had important backers. The standard-bearers of Chinese influence were the Soga clan, who had entrenched their position at court by a series of marriages with the imperial family. To bolster their position further and to lessen the influence of rivals who had the support of the old Shinto establishment, they took the radical step of embracing Buddhism, which was officially introduced to the Japanese court from Korea in the year 552.

At first the new religion failed to take on. Soon after its arrival, a deadly epidemic swept the country. The conservative faction lost no time in

Zen and Tea: A Meditative Combination

Under the influence of Zen Buddhism, the drinking of tea – in a ceremony called chanoyu – *became a contemplative ritual intended to clear the mind and refine the senses.*

Both tea and Zen were originally brought to Japan from China, where the drink was popular in monasteries as a promoter of good health and a stimulant to ward off fatigue during meditation. Its use spread among the aristocracy, who enjoyed tea-tastings in which the merits of different brews were compared. It was Zen monks such as Juko (1422–1502), an expert on Chinese art, who ritualized its use, linking it with meditation and aesthetics in a uniquely Japanese way.

As the tea ceremony or *chanoyu* evolved, it became an exercise in contemplative decorum in which the downing of the bitter-tasting infusion, made with green, unfermented leaves and whisked to a froth, played only a small part. Participants took time to appreciate the simple, seemingly artless utensils used in its preparation as well as to reflect on the artworks displayed in purpose-built teahouses, themselves models of unadorned architecture. In time, every step involved in the making and drinking of the tea was dictated by tradition, every gesture of host and guests calculated to soothe; the atmosphere was one of religious solemnity.

Even so, the endemic violence that rocked the country in those anarchic times sometimes disturbed even this sheltered world. Oda Nobunaga, the shogun who set in motion the re-uniting of the country, was ambushed by enemies while enjoying a tea ceremony in Kyoto's Honnoji Temple, and ritually disembowelled himself to evade capture and death. And the greatest of all tea-masters, Senno Rikyu (1522–91), was forced to commit suicide by Nobunaga's successor Hideyoshi, allegedly for refusing to send his daughter to provide for the great lord's pleasure.

The teahouse or *chashitsu* was the epitome of quiet understatement, deliberately creating a feeling of intimacy, equality and simplicity. A women's meal in a ceremonial tearoom, woodblock print by Toshikata, c.1900.

blaming the disaster on the imported faith, which was officially proscribed; a huge image of the Buddha that had been expensively imported from Korea was mutilated and thrown into a canal.

But the Soga persevered. Twenty years later, they received imperial permission to try again. A Korean monk who had settled in Japan was persuaded to take up his old calling, and he enrolled three girls as nuns. From these humble beginnings, the new faith grew. As it spread, hostility to it also increased, erupting eventually into full-scale civil war. But the Soga emerged from the conflict victorious, and the future of Buddhism in Japan was thereby assured.

So too was the influence of China. In 592 the victorious chief of the Soga clan had his niece declared empress, while real power devolved on a nephew by another marriage, Prince Shotoku Taishi. For the next three decades Shotoku devoted himself single-mindedly to the cause of reform, drawing his inspiration unambiguously from the mainland power. In 607 he sent a large delegation to the court of the Sui emperor, setting a pattern that was to be repeated many times over the next three centuries. By it, many of Japan's best and brightest came to view a visit to the mainland to study the achievements of Chinese civilization as a part of their preparation for assuming positions of power back home.

In the next century, Chinese influence took concrete form in the *Taika* or "Great Change", a series of measures announced in 646 that consciously sought to model Japanese society on that of China. They established a centralized administration on Confucian lines and theoretically put all lands in the hands of the emperor. At the same time, a census of estates was taken to improve government efficiency, and new taxes were

imposed. The process was completed by the establishment in AD710 of a fixed capital at Nara – previously power had resided wherever the emperor chose to build a palace – and the preparation, on royal command, of the *Kojiki* (AD712) and the *Nihongi* or *Nihonshoki* (AD720), official chronicles of Japanese history and mythology shaped to establish the unquestioned primacy of the imperial house (see box, page 15).

The Nara period marked the crest of the Chinese wave in Japanese affairs. In the administration, records were meticulously kept by Chinese-style bureaucrats in Chinese characters; at court, elegant noblemen in palaces laid out on Chinese lines studied Chinese art and literature and wore mandarins' robes. The infatuation was to have long-lasting effects: even the very word Japan by which the nation is known in the English-speaking world derives ultimately – due to the shared written character – from the Chinese *jihpen* rather than from the Japanese *nippon*, although both mean "land of the rising sun".

In religious terms, the hand of China was felt in the spread of Buddhism, which deeply entrenched itself in Japan at this time. The island kingdom became a magnet for priests and monks from the mainland, while many Japanese converts went there to study under local masters before returning to their homeland to spread the word. One telling reason for their undoubted success lay in Shinto's aversion to all contact with death; seeking comfort in their bereavement, many mourners turned for solace to the new faith, which established something of a monopoly in the care of the sick and the burial of the dead.

Before long the two religions came to an understanding that was to survive almost unchallenged for the next 1,000 years. After the military

17

defeat of their supporters by the Soga clan, the Shinto priesthood decided to seek accommodation with the new faith rather than continuing to resist it. The rest of the population followed suit, and the two religions entered a period of peaceful co-existence that has survived to the present day.

The mood of tolerance was symbolized in the year 735, when Emperor Shomu determined to erect a giant statue of the Buddha as an offering from the nation to help ward off a smallpox epidemic that was sweeping the land. At first there was some doubt whether the adherents of Shinto would support the move, so a priest was dispatched to Amaterasu's shrine at Ise to find out if the goddess approved the work. After seven days and nights of prayer, he reported back that the goddess herself had spoken to him. She had repeated a verse from a Chinese poem to the effect that she welcomed the plan as eagerly as

she would a boat at a river crossing or a torch on a dark night. The project went ahead, and when the sixteen-metre-high image was installed in the Golden Hall of Nara's Todaji monastery, Shinto priests petitioned successfully to have the shrine of their own war-god Hachiman moved into the grounds to serve as its spiritual guardian.

Monasteries were, in fact, another novelty introduced by Buddhism, and their rapid spread soon showed that they they filled a deep spiritual need. By the start of the Nara period there were already more than 500 in Japan, and the number grew rapidly. So did their size; over the years the largest developed into complex communities as big as small towns. As they expanded, so did their political influence, and before long they had created a power base that rivalled the court itself.

As such, they hastened the demise of Nara as the imperial seat. After just seventy-four years' use,

TIMELINE	28,000BC–AD500	AD500–1200
An island nation with a distinctive and ancient mythology, Japan for many centuries looked to the older civilization of China for its inspiration. When Chinese influence waned, society gradually settled into a feudal order in which the imperial court exercised symbolic authority while real power lay in the hands of hardened fighting men. A similarly contradictory pattern of refinement and violence marked the nation's cultural life. Today, the emperor is traditionally believed to occupy the Chrysanthemum Throne as Amaterasu's direct descendant, a fact which lends Japanese mythology an intriguing edge, for it is very much a living tradition.	**c.28,000BC** First settlers may have arrived across land-bridges connected to Korea and Siberia. **c.10,000BC** Palaeolithic groups were making use of chipped stone. **c.8000BC** Peoples of the Jomon culture supplanted the Neolithic occupants. The Ainu, a Caucasoid people from Siberia, also arrived. **c.660BC** First Emperor Jimmu Tenno traditionally said to have ascended the throne and led the imperial clan to the Yamato plain on Honshu. **c.300BC** Rice cultivation may have reached Kyushu with the Yayoi, who brought paddy-field techniques pioneered in southern China. They also introduced both bronze and iron concurrently to the islands. **c.AD1** The Yayoi spread to Honshu. During their ascendancy Japan changed from a society of hunter-gatherers to one of settled agricultural communities, divided by its geography into competing clans led by its rulers. **c.50** Shrine to Amaterasu founded at Ise. **c.300** The Kofun or Burial Mound era began, with large tomb complexes built. **c.300–400** Rise to pre-eminence of the clans controlling the Yamato plain. **391–405** Chinese literature and script introduced to Japan's illiterate elite. *A clay Doggu figure in the form of a human-animal torso. Middle-Late Jomon, 350–250BC.*	**552–572** Buddhism officially introduced to the Soga court. Soga victory in a civil war assured the future of Buddhism in Japan. **607** Japanese imperial delegation to China's court set a pattern for the next 300 years. **646** Chinese influence took form in the *Taika* or "Great Change", a series of measures that consciously sought to model Japan on China. **710** Nara founded as Japan's permanent capital. **712** The *Kojiki* was compiled. **720** The *Nihongi* was completed. **784** New purpose-built imperial capital to the north of Nara was decided upon and called Heian, in later times to be known as Kyoto. **794–1185** The Heian era – a time of courtly refinement and artistic achievement. **894** Ties with China were formally severed and were not resumed for five centuries. **1156–85** Succession dispute led to the Fujiwara clan losing its grip. Seeking to fill the power vacuum, the Taira and Minamoto clans fought The Gempei War, 1180–85. **1185** Victorious Yoritomo retreated to Kamakura in the eastern Minamoto heartland and wielded power under the title of shogun, or imperial general. **1192** First shogunate established. The emperor ruled from Heian, but he did so with only formal trappings. Real power lay with the shogun.

the country's rulers decided to leave their purpose-built capital, largely to escape from the influence of the Buddhist clergy who had become firmly entrenched there. One monk by the name of Dokyo had insinuated himself, Rasputin-like, into the favours of a reigning empress, inveigling her into making him her chancellor and then scheming unsuccessfully to mount the throne itself. When his patron died soon afterwards, the monk was hastily exiled to a remote island. But the looming Buddhist presence remained, and it was enough to persuade the imperial court to find a new home. They eventually settled on a site approximately fifty kilometres to the north of Nara, where they established the new capital of Heian, in later times to be known as Kyoto.

Courtiers and Courtesans

The Heian era, from AD794 to 1185, was a time of growing self-confidence in which Japan learned to stand on its own feet and direct Chinese influence was finally laid to rest. The last of the great missions to the Tang court was dispatched in 838, at a time when the dynasty was starting to lose its grip. As the situation on the mainland deteriorated, relations between the two nations became steadily more strained. Ties were formally severed in 894 and were not resumed for five centuries.

By that time the Japanese court no longer felt the need to look anywhere but to itself for models of taste and sophistication. Their faces powdered fashionably white, the noblemen and women who crowded its halls, gardens and chambers described themselves as "cloud-dwellers" and devoted themselves to the cult of *miyabi*, or courtly refinement, in which the greatest virtues

A kakiemon model of a seated tiger, late 17th century.

1200–1650

1268 Mongol leader Kublai Khan prepared to launch an invasion.
1274 Some 30,000 Mongol soldiers landed on the coast of Kyushu but were prevented from advancing by determined Japanese resistance.
1281 Further Mongol invasion fleet smashed by a storm with severe loss of men. The Japanese called the typhoon a *kamikaze* or divine wind.
1333 Kamakura captured by rivals and burned.
1336 Ashikaga clan's shogun Takaiyi exercised power from Kyoto as the shogunate struggled to prevent a descent into feudal anarchy.
1467 With all pretence of central authority gone, the Warring States Period was marked by endemic civil war lasting more than a century.
1542–43. The first Europeans – merchants from Portugal – arrived off Kyushu. They brought firearms and the Christian religion.
1549 Francis Xavier became the first Christian missionary to proselytize Japan. The religion made headway in Kyushu.
1560–97 Ashikaga clan, via *daimyo* Oda Nobunaga, attempted to reunify the country. His work was completed by Toyotomi Hideyoshi.
1597 Hideyoshi suddenly began a persecution of Christianity that was to extirpate the faith throughout the nation within four decades.
1598 A brief war after Hideyoshi's death was won by Ieyasu, leader of the Tokugawa clan.
1603 Tokugawa shogunate reorganized Japanese society on feudal lines, from its capital at Edo.
1639 Japan isolated from the rest of the world.

1650–PRESENT DAY

A highly ornately crafted iron tsuba of the acclaimed Nara school, 19th century.

1853 Four American warships arrived under Commodore Perry.
1868 Tokugawa era ended by radical reformers acting in the emperor's name. Emperor Mutsuhito's court moved to Edo (Tokyo), taking the name Meiji.
1872 Shinto adopted as the state religion.
1876 Samurai position as a special class ended.
1894–95 Japan succeeded in the Sino-Japanese War
1905 Japan decisively defeated Russia's navy at Tsushima in the Korea Strait.
1937–45 Period of militant nationalism ended in ultimate defeat and the dropping of atomic bombs on the cities of Hiroshima and Nagasaki.
1945–52 Japan occupied by Allied forces.
1946 Emperor publicly renounced all claims to divinity in a radio broadcast, thereby ending a tradition going back more than 1,000 years.
1982 Just 30 years after being virtually destitute, Japan became the second-biggest economy in the world, after the United States.

great estates, the revenues of which served to support the absentee landowners in their glittering ceremonial round. Real power in the provinces devolved on the estate managers, tough, practical men who relied on the support of armed retainers known as *bushi* to maintain order and put down banditry. As for the work of tending the land, that fell to the peasantry who were for the most part treated with a disdain bordering on contempt by those who lived off their efforts.

The harshness of many people's lives proved fertile ground for the further spread of Buddhism, which extended its popular appeal in the Heian period through a variety of new sects (see box, page 33). All offered the possibility of personal salvation, helping to plug another gap in Shintoism, which had little to offer its adherents in the afterlife; but they differed on the best routes to attain enlightenment. So the Tendai ("Heavenly Terrace") cult, established by the monk Saicho early in the ninth century, emphasized study of the sacred text known as the *Lotus Sutra*. Shingon ("True Word"), founded by Saicho's contemporary Kukai, concentrated on the repetition of certain sacred formulae passed on in secret to initiates. The Jodo ("Pure Land") movement later gained widespread popular support by promising its followers a blissful future in the western paradise of that name if they devoted themselves wholeheartedly to worship of the Amida Buddha.

When it was introduced to Japan in the twelfth century, the Pure Land sect's message fell on receptive ears, for by that time the Heian world was starting to fall apart. Over the centuries the imperial government's economic base had been weakened as various powerful groups – leading noblemen, Buddhist monasteries, Shinto shrines – won tax exemptions for their estates. Attempts to redistribute the land to those who worked it – a

were elegance and restraint. Art flourished as never before, and a great age of literature dawned. Two of its chief proponents were women: Sei Shonagon, whose *Pillow Book* was a discursive literary jotter, as revealing in its snobberies as in its refinements, and Lady Murasaki who in *The Tale of Genji* wrote a work often described as the world's first great novel.

While the aristocracy preened and paraded at Heian, the rest of Japanese society went about its business in the provinces little noticed by its rulers. The countryside was divided up into some 5,000

measure foreseen in the *Taika* reforms – had long been given up. And the provincial administration had also fallen into purely local hands as individual warlords looked to their own soldiery to maintain their position rather than to the pronouncements of the emperor's ministers.

The Shoguns Take Power

Events came to a head when the Fujiwara clan, which had long dominated Japanese politics, lost its grip following a disputed imperial succession in the mid-twelfth century, leaving a power vacuum at the centre of the administration. Two rival groups – the Taira of western Honshu and the Minamoto from the east of the island – sought to fill it. Almost inevitably, it was not long before their warriors came to blows.

At first victory went to the Taira. Under their leader Kiyomori they took a bloody revenge on their adversaries, condemning most of their leaders to death. Among the victims were fifty courtiers, the first members of the emperor's retinue to be executed in more than 350 years. It was a sign that the old court world was starting to fall apart.

But the Minamoto had lost a battle rather than the war. In his hour of triumph, Kiyomori made the mistake of alienating many influential people by his pride and the arrogance of his Taira followers. The Minamoto regrouped and, following Kiyomori's death in 1181, were able to gain the upper hand in a fiercely fought civil war.

The climax came four years later in a naval battle at Dannoura in the strait between Honshu and Kyushu, when the Taira were routed. The grandmother of the seven-year-old Emperor Antoku, a Taira supporter, committed suicide on the spot, jumping into the sea with the infant ruler in her arms. Amaterasu's sword, part of the imperial regalia passed down through the generations, went with her; so would the goddess's mirror, except that the lady-in-waiting who was carrying it was prevented from following her mistress overboard when a Minamoto arrow pinned her court robes to the deck.

A new emperor duly ascended the throne in Heian, but the balance of power had nonetheless fundamentally changed. After the battle the victorious Minamoto commander, Yoritomo, was given the title of shogun, or "imperial general". But unlike Kiyomori he did not make the mistake of playing the courtier. Instead he retired to the small town of Kamakura – today in the Tokyo suburbs – 800 kilometres from Heian in the eastern lands where his power base lay. There he set up an administrative network that in time became known as the *bakufu* or "tent government" – the term applied to the headquarters of an army in the field.

Large cypress-wood sculpture of Amida Buddha, the Buddha of Immeasurable or Pure Light, who resides in Gokuraku Jodo. Late Heian period, 12th century.

In so doing, he set a pattern for the next 700 years of Japanese history. Throughout that time the emperor would continue to rule from Heian, or Kyoto as it in time came to be called, just as he had in the past. But he did so with only the formal trappings of authority – and even they were sometimes threadbare when money became tight. Meanwhile, real power was exercised by the shogun who ruled in his name. The militarization of Japanese society, previously latent, now became clear for all to see, as the generals appointed fellow-warriors to provincial governorships, backed up by stewards administering the great estates with the help of armies of battle-hardened retainers.

Yet even if the mailed fist was now more in evidence than the gloved hand, society at large drew some real benefits from the new order. In the early years at least, the shogun's administration was decisive and effective where the Heian emperors' had too often been vacillating and ineffectual. Estates that had long been exempt from taxation now had to make a contribution to the running of the country. Law and order were enforced, and a serious attempt was made to extend the benefits of improved government beyond the confines of the ruling class. The Kamakura ethos was summed up in the Joei Formulary, a collection of rules and legal precepts that aimed to simplify the administration of justice and that stressed the importance of impartiality. The principles that it laid down were to remain the guiding lights of the Japanese legal system for the next 700 years.

The Rise of the Warrior Cult

The changed political atmosphere soon also made its influence felt in other spheres of Japanese life. Culturally, a new genre glorifying the exploits of military heroes made its appearance. Many of the tales had their roots in the struggle between the Taira and Minamoto clans. At first they circulated orally, recited aloud by story-tellers for an audience of warriors. In time, however, they were written down in the form of prose romances by scholarly compilers. Some of the tales embedded themselves deeply in the nation's store of legend.

The warriors left their mark in religious life, too. They were among the first enthusiasts for Zen Buddhism, which reached Japan at this time. They liked the anti-intellectualism of the new sect, as well as the emphasis it put on meditation and the use of shock tactics designed to surprise the adept into sudden enlightenment. At the same time, Shintoism was given a fillip by the activities of the

All the Mongol efforts to conquer Japan were repulsed. This picture scroll shows invasion junks being boarded; at right, one well-known warrior hero, Takezaki, is cutting an enemy's throat.

Watarai family, the hereditary guardians of Amaterasu's shrine at Ise. In a movement that became known as Watarai Shinto, they sought to revitalize the old faith by reaffirming the importance of purification rituals and of making an annual pilgrimage to Ise in order to attain spiritual advancement. The message struck home, and in the ensuing centuries the holy place regularly received more than half a million visitors a year.

As events turned out, Japan needed the benefits of orderly military rule more than anyone could have foreseen, for at the end of the thirteenth century it had to face the greatest threat to its existence since its history had begun. The Mongol hordes that had conquered much of Eurasia had seized control of China, and in 1268 their leader, Kublai Khan, sent envoys demanding the payment of tribute and submission to his rule. The imperial court prepared a weak reply, but the shogun would have none of it, preferring instead uncompromising rejection of the demand.

The nation then set about mobilizing to resist the expected invasion, which duly followed in 1274. Some 30,000 enemy soldiers landed on the northern coast of Kyushu, but were prevented from advancing further into the country by determined Japanese resistance. After a week of stalemate a storm blew up, and the Korean sailors accompanying the force persuaded the Mongols to

re-embark. It proved a costly decision, for many boats were wrecked on the journey back to the mainland and thousands of men were drowned.

Kublai Khan, however, was not prepared to accept defeat. He sent further envoys reiterating his demands. The Japanese response was unambiguous; they sent back the emissaries' severed heads. Kublai's answer was to dispatch two separate fleets to Japan, this time carrying between them a staggering 144,000 men. Again the invaders were restricted to a narrow beachhead by determined Japanese resistance. And once more a storm came to the defenders' aid, smashing the Mongols' ships and forcing them to withdraw for good with the loss of more than half their men. The Japanese called the typhoon a *kamikaze* or "divine wind", a term borrowed by suicide bombers confronting another imminent invasion 664 years later.

The victory of 1281 was the Kamakura shogunate's finest hour, but it was achieved on Pyrrhic terms. The expense of defending the realm had drained the exchequer dry. The shoguns no longer had spare land with which to buy support from provincial warlords. Discontent spread as Yoritomo's system of government broke down completely. In 1333 Kamakura itself was captured by rivals and burned down.

Yet the shogunate itself survived, though in a weakened form. Under the Ashikaga clan, the military governors struggled with increasing difficulty to prevent the country from descending into feudal anarchy, with power devolving entirely on

The Japanese warrior was expected to be able to loose arrows on horseback and to this end stirrups were devised which enabled him to stand while in the saddle. Functionally perfect, they did not change over the centuries. Iron and silver horseman's stirrups, 17th century.

local overlords seeking to advance their own interests. It was a losing battle. The final debacle came in 1467, when rival factions confronted one another in the streets of Kyoto itself. By the time the fighting was over, the imperial city was a ruin and all pretence of authority had disappeared. Civil war spread across the land.

The Samurai Saga

Yet, oddly, the fabric of society did not break down. The peasantry continued to till the land as they had always done, and in the towns that were growing up across the nation crafts and trade were flourishing. Most of the fighting was done by bands of professional warriors, the descendants of the *bushi* of earlier times. By now they were known as samurai, literally "serving men". Many of them were younger sons of noble families, for by ancient tradition such individuals lost their status as aristocrats after six gen-

erations and had to find employment. They did so by attaching themselves as military retainers to the *daimyo* – the owners of the great estates – pledging absolute loyalty to their masters and often being granted their own land in return. Successful samurai had residences protected by moats and stockades that enclosed stables, storehouses and servants' quarters as well as their own dwellings.

Divided up between rival *daimyo* recognizing only nominal fealty to a largely powerless emperor in Kyoto, sixteenth-century Japan was a vibrant, dangerous place that was surprisingly open to new influences. Many of these came from Europe, which was in its great phase of post-Renaissance expansion. The first Europeans to set foot on Japanese soil were Portuguese merchants, who arrived on an island off Kyushu in 1542 or 1543. With them they brought firearms, which quickly changed the face of Japanese warfare.

Another import was the Christian religion. Francis Xavier became the first missionary to proselytize Japan on his arrival in 1549. Others followed, making considerable headway in the southern island of Kyushu.

Meanwhile other forces were at work that would eventually lead to the reunification of the country. The first steps were taken by an ambitious and determined *daimyo* named Oda Nobunaga, who seized Kyoto in 1568 and by the time of his death in 1582 had brought much of central Japan under his control. His work was then taken up by Toyotomi Hideyoshi, the son of a common soldier in Nobunaga's pay, who had himself appointed regent by the emperor, and in a series of battles managed to impose his rule on the entire country.

As the true ruler of Japan, Hideyoshi proved effective but intemperate, given to sudden rages and abrupt decisions. Possibly with a mind to

Eighteenth-century painted screen depicting Japanese musicians welcoming Portuguese missionaries. The arrival of Europeans prompted an entire genre of similar paintings.

most senior government positions. Below them were the peasantry, their lives ruled by heavy taxes and draconian regulations, and on the lowest rungs came craftsmen and traders. These last were despised as money-grubbers by the warrior elite, but in fact many took advantage of the long Tokugawa peace to make substantial fortunes by providing the goods that the *daimyo* and samurai wanted.

In this closely ordered society one potentially disruptive element remained a thorn in the shoguns' flesh: foreigners, who were coming to Japan in increasing numbers. In response, the nation's rulers came to a startling decision: to get rid of them entirely. In the first decades of the seventeenth century, a series of decrees effectively cut the country off from the rest of the world. In 1636, Japanese were forbidden to travel abroad on pain of death; three years later, all non-Japanese were expelled. The only exceptions were a number of Chinese traders and some Dutch merchants, who were allowed to make a couple of visits annually to the island of Deshima in Nagasaki harbour.

However drastic their methods, the Tokugawa shoguns did succeed in giving the strife-torn nation 250 years of domestic peace. But they also effectively cut Japan off from the rest of the world at a time when it was being transformed by dramatic intellectual and technological change. The result was that when outside powers finally forced their way into the Tokugawa cocoon, initially in the form of four American warships which arrived in 1853 under the command of Commodore Matthew C. Perry, the country's rulers were completely unprepared to meet them.

keeping the newly unemployed samurai occupied, he ordered an abortive invasion of Korea that cost many thousands of lives. Although he had previously had friendly relations with the Christians, he suddenly in 1597 ordered the torture and execution of seven missionaries and nineteen of their followers, starting a persecution that over the next forty years was to extirpate the faith throughout the nation.

A brief civil war followed his death in 1598. It was won by Ieyasu, the leader of the Tokugawa clan which was to rule Japan for the next two and a half centuries. In the wake of the troubles of the recent past, stability was very much the order of the day, and the Tokugawa shoguns set about reorganizing Japanese society on remorselessly feudal lines. In future there were to be four classes, with the samurai warriors at the top; in effect they became a hereditary elite, occupying

So hesitant and unconvincing was the Tokugawa government's response to the challenge thrown down by Commodore Perry and to the "unequal treaties" that the United States and other foreign powers subsequently imposed that the regime collapsed within fifteen years of the ships' arrival. The instigators of its overthrow were young radicals obsessed with the need to restore the nation's pride. Seizing control of the imperial palace in Kyoto in 1868, they proclaimed an end to the shogunate in the name of the fifteen-year-old Emperor Mutsuhito and the restoration of imperial rule. Then they moved the young ruler and his court from Kyoto to the city of Edo, redubbed Tokyo, "the eastern capital". The reign-title under which Mutsuhito governed was also changed, to Meiji or "enlightened rule". A new beginning was to be made.

Modern Times

The gospel of the Meiji reformers was modernization, for they were convinced that Japan had fallen dangerously behind the West. And so they set about catching up on two centuries of progress in the shortest possible time. In the same spirit in which Prince Shotoku had sent envoys to China more than a millennium earlier, they now dispatched delegations to tour the principal European capitals, notebooks at the ready to take down details of everything they saw. Then they set about remodelling the nation, first dismantling the old Tokugawa caste system and then establishing new or revitalized institutions in its place. So ideas from Britain helped shape Japanese industry and

A Meiji three-case *inro* with an ivory netsuke. Many fine pieces of craftsmanship were produced in this period of resurgent Japan's fortunes, as the country underwent a period of social and economic modernization.

the Imperial Navy; France and Germany provided models for the new military establishment and a reformed school system.

Yet the Meiji reforms were always a balancing act between old and new, and in religious affairs the new rulers looked back to the most ancient traditions of Shintoism. They saw in the indigenous faith a beacon of stability for the population in a rapidly changing world. It was to serve as a prop of nationhood that, together with veneration of the emperor that it deified, would give modern Japan continuity with its past and provide a focus for the nationalism that inspired them. In so doing, they virtually reinvented Shinto, turning it for the first time into an organized religion with a recognized hierarchy of priests and gods. They also transformed its status, making it the state faith and relegating Buddhism, which had effectively held that position in Tokugawa times, to a subordinate role.

The success of the Meiji reforms was dramatically displayed in 1905 when Japan, which had already successfully confronted China in the Sino-Japanese War of 1894–95, took on Russia, decisively defeating the great European power's naval might at the Battle of Tsushima in the Korea Strait. But the militant nationalism that these victories inspired was to be the nation's eventual undoing. Initial military successes in China in the 1930s and in World War II gave way ultimately to defeat and the trauma of the dropping of atomic bombs on the cities of Hiroshima and Nagasaki. The subsequent Japanese surrender and the occupation of the islands by Allied forces was an

Emperor Akihito in 1990 following his accession to the Chrysanthemum Throne after the death of his father, Hirohito. The office and its attendant rituals affirm the enduring link between the imperial lineage and the ancient gods of Japan.

unprecedented disaster for a nation that had never before in its history been successfully invaded, at least since prehistoric times.

Despite the apocalyptic fears of many Japanese at the time, the experience of defeat turned out to be relatively benign. The occupying authorities put through a radical programme of democratic reforms that would probably have been impossible for any Japanese government subject to the pressure of vested interests. Universal suffrage was introduced and a programme of land reform undertaken. The emperor was retained as a national figurehead, though he was stripped of all political power. In addition, he publicly renounced all claims to divinity in a 1946 radio broadcast, thereby ending a tradition that had endured for well over 1,000 years.

Economically the nation bounced back from virtual destitution with extraordinary speed, and within thirty years of the ending of the Allied occupation in 1952 Japan was boasting a gross national product second only to that of the United States in the non-Communist world. Against all expectations, the prostrate nation of 1945 had turned out to be the post-war world's greatest success story.

Yet even in the new Japan of compact cars, camcorders and other high-technology gadgetry, the old myths have not been forgotten. The Meiji reformers used them consciously to foster nationalism, and certain conservative forces in politics and the Shinto priesthood would still like to put them to similar use to this day. Yet for many Japanese, the stories have no political connotations, being simply part of an inheritance of shared memories that stretches back even beyond the limits of the nation's recorded history.

Meanwhile for the rest of the world, no such ambiguities need apply. The gods and demons, angry ghosts and spirit maidens that populate the magic realms of Japanese myth fit naturally into a global heritage of folklore that transcends national cultures and boundaries. In that sense, the myths belong not just to Japan but to the whole world.

27

GRAIN OF THE GODS

Rice culture has shaped the Japanese as a people. The ancient stories relate how Susano despoiled the divine rice fields in his contest with Amaterasu (see page 40), while one of the most important rituals remaining today is *taue* or rice planting. Over the long course of Japan's history, *go-han* or "honourable rice" has been ever-present: it was the main offering to the gods; taxes were levied in rice payments; a samurai's status was measured by the size of his annual rice allotment; the rice god, Inari, is one of the most venerated of all the deities; and since the first century BC rice has been the country's principal crop. Rice wine or sake features strongly and auspiciously in myths and in modern ceremonies – drinking it is a way of sharing and communing with the gods.

Top: Black lacquer sake bottle, 18th century. Sake or rice wine has been brewed for several millennia. In myth it serves a purifying role and is used as a votive offering. Its auspicious associations survive at weddings when bride and groom take three sips of sake from three lacquered cups.

Above: The Second War between Mochi and Sake, part of a triptych by Hiroshige, 1843–45. *Mochi* is rice cake eaten at New Year and served with tea. Sake is often accompanied with seafood to sharpen its bland taste. The artist suggests a contest between the two rivals.

Above: Harvesting work in the rice paddy at Yamagata. There is a Japanese expression, "Blessed is the nation whose ruler is a farmer" – for it is believed that there is no healthier labour. Rice cultivation, the life of the nation, is considered sacred work in Japan. The emperor himself still conducts one rice-planting ritual every year, when sake is offered to the field god amid much festivity.

Left: Ivory *okimono* or ornament of rice sellers, *c.*1900. For merchants such as these Inari was a particularly venerated figure, for he was not only the rice deity but also the god of business and patron of general prosperity.

Right: Fox messenger figures guard the Inari shrine at Fushimi, near Kyoto, the largest of more than 40,000 dedicated to the rice god across Japan – there is even one at Ise.

A UNIVERSE OF GODS

When the Shinto deity Izanagi returned from a fruitless voyage to the underworld in pursuit of Izanami, he performed ritual ablutions to purify himself of the lingering stain of that dark place. He washed in the middle of a river and the impurities on his body formed the god Yasomaga-tsubi ("Eighty Evils of the Body"); then he gave issue to two other gods who would remedy the evil performed by this one. He bathed in different parts of the sea and produced two gods of the seabed, two divinities of the middle waters and two guardians of the restless surface waters. A host of other deities were brought into being as he continued to purify himself – most notably, the great Shinto sun goddess, Amaterasu, who emerged when he washed his left eye (see page 37).

The Shinto pantheon boasts gods and goddesses almost without number. Ancient texts refer to 800 deities, but in Japanese mythology the number eight (*ya*) is a sacred one meaning simply "many". The early Japanese revered objects of particular beauty or power, or of unusual size or shape. Rivers, waterfalls, mountains, boulders, animals, trees, grasses and rice paddies all had their resident *kami* or "beings of higher place". Ancestors could also become *kami* – a word sometimes used to identify the vital quality that makes an object or creature distinctively itself, the force of life that made it worthy of worship within the animistic Shinto faith. Diminutive sanctuaries called *hokora* were created in honour of the innumerable local *kami*.

Kami also took human form, but were invisible to ordinary people. They were divided into *amutsu-kami*, the "heavenly deities", and *kunitsu-kami*, "gods of the earthly realm". Higher, celestial deities such as Amaterasu were powerful but not omnipotent. They could not see events unfolding in the human world and had to use go-betweens to find out what was happening there. Nor could they see the future; they had to practise divination rituals to discover what was to come. By venerable tradition each god had two souls: the *arami-tama* was aggressive and the *nigimi-tama* was peace-loving. A deity would behave in starkly different ways, depending on which soul was in control at a given time. Even the god Susano, the very incarnation of riotous dissolution, had a gentle as well as a violent soul. Accordingly, Susano sometimes performed good deeds – such as when he saved Kusanada-hime ("Rice Paddy Princess") from the eight-tailed, eight-headed dragon that had been preying on her family (see pages 54–55).

Opposite: Kami were numinous spirit forces residing in the many places and things of the natural world, including humans. Pine tree on a rock at Kiri-Kiri, Iwate.

Below: The cockerel was the sacred bird of Amaterasu, the sun goddess, and it loudly welcomed each new sunrise. Sword guard or *tsuba*, 19th century.

The Shape of the Cosmos

In Japanese mythology, the cosmos took form spontaneously from chaos. The primeval universe was a fluid, seething mass in the shape of a giant egg. The lighter elements floated upwards and formed Takama-no-hara (the "High Plain of Heaven"), the abode of the gods, while the heavier ones settled and became the solid Earth.

Then, from a white cloud, emerged three sky *kami*. The first-born was Amenominakanusi ("Lord of the Centre of Heaven"), next was Takamimusubi ("August High Producer") and then Kamimusubi ("August Divine Producer"). Below, the Earth had not taken shape, for it was in constant motion like a darting fish or a patch of oil floating on the ocean. Yet from it sprang the first plant, a translucent reed shoot that forced its way up to the endless sky. There it became Umasiasikabipikodi ("Pleasant Prince Elder of the Reed Shoot") and Amenotokotati ("Everlasting Heaven Stander"). Now there were five divinities inhabiting the wide spaces of the sky. All were invisible, fluid spirits without physical form.

The five were followed by seven further generations of deities, each appearing in male-female pairs as brother and sister, husband and wife. The last of these was the couple Izanagi and Izanami (see pages 34–35).

There are many different genealogies of the first gods, given in ancient sources such as the *Kojiki* and *Nihongi*. In the forms that have survived, Japanese creation myths appear to have been influenced by Chinese tradition. Scholars of Shinto argue that the primeval division of the universe into lighter and heavier elements is an alien element. In Chinese stories the universe came into being when primordial chaos divided into its complementary principles of yin

A legendary *tengu* emerging from an egg. The Japanese concept of the primordial universe as a vast egg may have originated further afield, in China, India or Central Asia.

and yang. Some scholars believe that it is only with the exploits of Izanagi and Izanami that the myths reflect authentic, ancient Japanese tradition.

Cosmology

Gods continued to be created and the vast population of *kami* was divided into celestial divinities, *amutsu*, and earthly ones, *kunitsu*. The High Plain of Heaven supported a fertile landscape filled with blossoming trees and stern mountains – a fragrant territory like that of parts of Japan itself. Across it ran a wide river, Amano-gawa, through whose twinkling waters a bed of pebbles could be seen. From Earth up to Heaven above there once rose a walkway or bridge, Ama-no-Hashidate. But the bridge disintegrated on a day of angry winds, tumbling into the sea far below and creating an isthmus to the west of Kyoto that is celebrated for its wild beauty.

The Earth was called the Central Land of the Reed Plain. Deep beneath it lay Yomi, the dark land of the dead, where demons congregated, living in palaces or humble cottages according to their station in that world. The inhabitants of this underground hell were not paying the price for past sins: in the Shinto tradition there was no conception of a place of punishment after the death of the body; this came into Japan with Buddhism.

A Multitude of Worlds

Japan's Buddhist movements believed that the universe held worlds beyond number, populated by harmful or helpful spirits. While Shinto promised neither punishment nor reward after death, Buddhists could look forward to one of many paradises provided by Buddhas to save their faithful followers from the cycle of rebirth.

Standing sentinel over the universe to vanquish demons were four guardians, each of whom was concerned with a quarter of the cosmos: in the east was Jikoku ("Watchman of the Lands"), while the west was protected by Komoku ("Widely Seeing"); in the north stood Bishamon ("Widely Hearing") and in the south arose Zocho ("Patron of Growth").

Different paradises were associated with the numerous Buddhist sects, each of which had its own Butsu or Buddha. The largest was the Tendai school founded by Saicho at Mount Hiei in the late eighth century. Its paradise was Ryoju-sen, a Japanese form of Vulture Peak, a mountain in India. There, by tradition, Shakyamuni (Shaka-nyorai was the Japanese name for the Buddha) preached the sermon that was recorded in the *Lotus Sutra*, a Buddhist scripture best known in Japan through Tendai and the later creed of the thirteenth-century monk Nichiren. This paradise could be reached by Buddhists before death by meditating on the truth of the Lotus.

The glories of Gokuraku Jodo ("Western Paradise"), given form by Buddha Amida, were often celebrated and were well known to Japanese devotees of Jodo, the Pure Land tradition. There,

jewels adorned the ranks of trees that ranged in orderly lines along the mountainside, and colourful, singing birds created a celestial harmony. On a deep pond brimming with ambrosia floated sacred lotus plants. Caressed by breezes, the Butsu and his followers rested serenely on the soil; above, angels released flower petals onto them from the blessed air.

The twelfth-century monk Honen, a former Tendai devotee, taught that entry was open to anyone who devoutly repeated *nembutsu* in praise of the Amida.

A third paradise, Tosotsu-ten ("Paradise of Contentment"), belonged to Buddha Miroku (or Maitreya), who is destined to come to Earth far in the future. Devotees believed that Tosotsu-ten lay in the celestial realm; from time to time believers were transported there in a vision.

Bishamon, guardian of the north. Wooden statue, 18th century.

33

Begetting the World

The seventh august generation of celestial deities to stand forth on the High Plain of Heaven were Izanagi ("He Who Invites") and Izanami ("She Who Invites"). Their divine destiny was to establish the fair, sea-kissed islands of Yamato (Japan) in the unruly waters far below.

The older sky *kami* gave Izanagi and Izanami a magnificent spear with a bright blade and cold handle of sea coral adorned with glittering jewels. The couple ventured forth onto the majestic rainbow known as the Floating Bridge of Heaven and Izanagi used the spear to agitate the restless ocean on whose surface the shapeless Earth still floated like oil. The waters began to thicken and when Izanagi lifted the spear a drop from it solidified, forming Onogoro ("Spontaneously Coagulated"), the very first island.

Divine Union

Down the steep and elegant staircase of the heavenly rainbow came Izanagi and Izanami to test the land. They built a sacred pillar and a fine dwelling place worthy of august *kami* such as they.

Then god and goddess looked upon one another with desire. In some accounts they did not know how to achieve sexual union until they saw a pair of wagtails shaking their tails energetically; Izanagi and Izanami copied the birds and joined their bodies together. In the version recounted in the *Kojiki*, Izanami told her brother-husband that there was one place in which her body was lacking; he replied that his body had a place where there was too much and they agreed to unite these two parts. Their divine intention was to bring forth new lands and new generations of divinities from their partnership.

They devised a propitious ritual to celebrate their marriage: she would circle the holy pillar from the right while he did so from the left; when they met they would be one. When Izanami rounded the pillar and encountered Izanagi she exclaimed in pleasure at the sight of him. He,

seeing her beauty, also cried out with delight – but he reminded her that it was improper for a member of her sex to speak first in this way.

The Progeny of Izanagi and Izanami

The first fruit of their union was not happy. Izanami gave birth to a malformed child shaped like a leech or jellyfish. The troubled couple laid the infant tenderly in a boat of reeds and set it floating on the water.

Sometimes the leech child is associated with the god Hiruko; in one Japanese account Hiruko's name is said to mean "child-leech". Hiruko may have been a sun god whose cult was replaced by that of Amaterasu when the Yamato clan achieved dominance (see page 13).

Izanagi and Izanami climbed to the wide High Plain of Heaven to try to discover the reason for the monstrous birth. After performing divination, the other sky deities revealed that the cause was the polluting effect of Izanami's error in speaking before her husband during their ritual at the pillar. So the couple returned and repeated the ceremony, only this time, Izanami kept her silence until spoken to by her husband.

Now their lovemaking bore fruit in the shape of the eight largest islands of Japan. At the same time the smaller islands of the archipelago and foreign lands far and wide formed from bubbles in the unruly ocean. When Izanagi saw the islands swathed in fragrant morning mists he inhaled deeply and cleared the air – his breath became the deity of the wind. Hunger troubled the couple, so they created the *kami* of rice. They made the gods and goddesses of the mountains, of the sea, of rivermouths and of trees.

But when Izanami came to give birth to the fire god, Kagutsuchi, she was terribly burned. Izanagi gasped with horror to see his beloved cast down, beyond comfort, on the ground. He realized she would die and railed bitterly against her cruel fate. But even her death and his furious grief resulted in the birth of many *kami*. The myth's many different versions give various names for these deities. According to one account, before she died Izanami gave issue to an earth goddess and a water goddess and to a deity named Wakamusubi ("Young Growth") from whose belly grew rice, corn, millet, hemp and pulse. Another account claims that poor Izanami vomited, spewing forth the goddess Kanayama ("Princess Metal Mountain"), and both her urine and excrement were also transformed into deities.

The tears shed by Izanagi in his anger also turned into gods and goddesses. Bitterly regretting the birth of Kagutsuchi who had deprived him of his beloved sister-wife, he drew his sword and sliced the child into three (some say, five) pieces – and each one became a god. The many drops of the child's blood that he spilled became stones in the wide river flowing across the High Plain of Heaven and can still be seen as the stars in the Milky Way. In another account the fire god's dismembered body became five great deities associated with mountains (see page 46).

Izanagi and Izanami stand on the Floating Bridge of Heaven. Izanagi is dipping his jewelled spear into the primeval ocean. Late 19th-century hanging scroll by Eitaku Kobayashi.

35

Journey to the Underworld

Izanagi, distraught with grief, determined to follow his beloved to Yomi, the "shadowy land of the dead". In the underworld he discovered a land not unlike that above, but a heavy gloom hung over everything like a pall. Although the inhabitants were accustomed to the darkness, for anyone used to the sun-ripened territory above, Yomi was a place of horror.

Izanagi could only drive his feet forward into those deathly shadows by remembering his wife's delicate form and graceful manner while alive. At length he discovered Izanami. He knew her by her voice, but he could not see her due to the darkness in that corner of Yomi. At once, in trembling tones, he begged her to return with him to the land above. But she spoke harshly to her husband, blaming him for having delayed in seeking her out; she had, she told him angrily, eaten the dark food of the underworld, thus bonding herself with the dead; she could no longer return to the land of the living.

Izanami said she was about to lie down to rest and begged her husband not to disturb her as she slept. But Izanagi, maddened by grief and angry at her refusal to return with him, waited until she was asleep, then took the comb with which he secured his long hair, broke off the end tooth and set it alight. His torch sent up a burst of light that startled the shadows and crowding demons, sending them scurrying.

He saw his wife's recumbent body in the gloom and, lifting the torch higher, was sickened to see Izanami as she had become in that place. For her body was swollen and rotting, home to crawling maggots; slavering over her were eight foul thunder gods, incarnations of the underground thunders heard in earthquakes.

Izanagi cried aloud with horror. Then when he could bear to look no more, he threw down the torch and ran, blundering into the thick and filthy darkness. He was pursued by Izanami's shrieking curses, for she had been woken by his shout of despair and was enraged and ashamed that he had exposed her to light. She sent eight wild *shikome* ("foul women") clamouring after him. Their keening threats and curses rang out in that cavernous place, making Izanagi's skin crawl with horror.

Brandishing his sword, Izanagi ran for his life. Then he stopped and flung his headdress down onto the mulchy ground. It became a bunch of black grapes on which the hideous women

Demonically depicted Raiden, one of the eight gods of thunder. His drum was used to beat out the terrifying noise of earthquakes as well as storms in the sky. Wood and ivory carving, early 19th century.

Heavenly Illumination

The Nihongi *features a variant myth of the creation of Amaterasu and Tsukiyomi in which Izanagi produced the* kami *of the sun, the moon and the underworld from mirrors prior to his first act of procreation with his sister-goddess.*

Izanagi stood alone in Onogoro and declared his intention to create offspring who would rule the world.

To this end he took a mirror of white copper in his left hand and, merely by gazing into it, divinely brought forth a deity named Ohohirume (probably a pseudonym for Amaterasu, for it means "Great Noon Female", a time when the sun is at the height of its power).

Then Izanagi lifted an identical mirror in his right hand and with his gaze gave form to Tsukiyomi. Using exactly the same mirror but this time looking sideways at it, he next created the god called Susano.

The first two divinities cast a bright light all about. Izanagi set them in the firmament to illumine the Earth far and wide: Tsukiyomi would shine with a pale light by night, while Ohohirume's fierce rays would be seen by day. But the third deity, Susano, proved almost at once to be dedicated to ruin, a

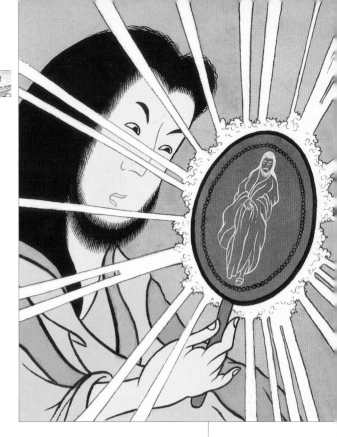

bringer of destruction. Therefore Izanagi dispatched him to govern the underworld of Yomi, home to foul hags and demons.

---

ravenously fell, but they consumed them almost at once and continued their pursuit. Then Izanagi threw down his comb which became a clump of bamboo shoots and delayed the harridans once more. Izanami, seeing this, herself gave chase.

Izanagi was now almost safe, for he had reached the boundary of Yomi. The *Nihongi* version recounts how he stopped to urinate against a tree, giving issue to a great river that delayed his pursuers still further. In another account he was chased by Yomi's infantrymen, but kept them at bay by throwing peaches that he found growing on his path. Then he took a boulder and used it to block the passage between the worlds of the living and the dead. He heard Izanami arrive panting on the other side, but she could not reach him.

The huge rock's cold weight lay between god and goddess as Izanagi declared that he would divorce Izanami. She answered that if that came to pass she would destroy 1,000 inhabitants of the land of the living every day. He furiously countered that he would give life to 1,500. And so it was that death came into the world; but men and women, protected by Izanagi, still prosper, for they bring more lives into the world than are lost to the cold fury of proud Izanami.

In the bright light on Earth Izanagi saw the polluting mark of the underworld on his skin. He threw down his staff, shoes and clothing in horror, and they became deities. He plunged into a sweetly flowing river and then the wide sea to purify himself. (By ancient tradition mourners at a Japanese funeral would ceremonially wash themselves to rid themselves of the taint of death.)

Later Izanagi bathed his left eye and the goddess Amaterasu came forth; from his right eye sprang the deity Tsukiyomi. He flooded his nose with waters in a bid to flush out the dread odour of the land below and in so doing he brought forth the god Susano.

Amaterasu and Susano

Izanagi was restored and cleansed by his ablutions after the horror of his ordeal in the underworld. Addressing himself to the principal deities to which he had given form, he took his precious and holy necklace and handed it to the goddess Amaterasu as a sign that she would have dominion over the sky as the sun goddess.

To pale-skinned Tsukiyomi Izanagi gave rule of the night sky and the moon. In this account, sun and moon were devoted wife and husband, but when Tsukiyomi killed the food goddess (see box, page 41) they fell out – and for this reason they are rarely seen together. Susano, meanwhile, became guardian of the restless seas, or in some accounts of the Earth (although he was later assigned the underworld as a punishment – see page 44).

Susano Climbs to Heaven

Amaterasu and Tsukiyomi, then, occupied their allotted stations on the wide High Plain of Heaven, but in the Central Land of the Reed Plain, as Earth was called, Susano caused nothing but trouble. Without stop he howled and railed against Izanagi; in some versions – which identify him as Lord of

the Earth – he neglected his duties, and the foliage drenching the steep mountainsides and the fair blossom on the clustering trees withered during his period of rule.

When Izanagi asked what was the matter, Susano loudly complained that his station on Earth was not to his liking, for his only desire was to follow his mother to the land below where she had perforce now to dwell. Angrily Izanagi granted his son's wish and banished him to Yomi.

Now Izanagi – his destiny fulfilled – elected to retire. One version has it that he climbed to Heaven and lived in close proximity to his daughter in the Palace of the Sun. Others say he took up residence at Taga on the island of Honshu, where he is still worshipped to this day.

Then Susano declared that, before descending to the land of the dead, he must climb to the

Echoes of an Ancient Sibling Struggle

Some scholars believe that the myth of Amaterasu's conflict with Susano may preserve the ancient memory of an actual struggle between a priestess and her brother in prehistoric Japan.

There is a record in the annals of the third-century-AD Chinese Wei dynasty of civil wars in Japan which followed the death of Himeko, priestess and queen of the kingdom of Yamato.

According to the Chinese historians, when Himeko's younger brother took the throne it sparked a conflict which was

ended only when Himeko's daughter took his place as ruler of her late mother's realm.

It is more likely, however, that the myth reflects a clan conflict in early Japan. Amaterasu was the great goddess of the Yamato clan and was revered as an ancestor of Japan's legendary first emperor, Jimmu. Susano, on

the other hand, was worshipped especially by the Yamato clan's enemies in the Izumo region. When the myths of Susano and Amaterasu were recorded, the Yamato clan had vanquished those in Izumo and were seeking to legitimize their superiority by establishing Amaterasu's seniority over Susano.

High Plain of Heaven in order to bid farewell to his fair sister Amaterasu. As Susano began the journey, his great and virile energy caused the vast seas to boil and the Earth to shudder and gape in a massive earthquake.

In Heaven above stood Amaterasu. Hearing the commotion and seeing Susano approaching through the tall clouds and shifting mists, she concluded – knowing all too well his violent temper – that her brother was coming to her with evil intent. Her face grew dark; she convinced herself that envy drove him to climb up to steal her celestial realm. Girding herself for grim battle, she tied up her hair and her skirts, winding the string of dark jewels around her head and wrists. Then, picking up her great quivers, her bow of war and her sword that glimmered with the light of Heaven, she stepped forth as a warrior. Her strength was so great that, when she stamped, her mighty legs sank into the ground as will a galloping stallion's into the foam at the ocean's edge.

Mount Fuji, the pre-eminent sacred peak in Japan, rises above autumnal suzuki grass, evoking an ancient image of the Central Land of the Reed Plain. Fujiyama or Fuji was also home to Sengen-Sama, goddess of blossoms.

The Competition of Procreation

Amaterasu challenged her brother in bold terms, but Susano reproached her, saying that he came only to pay a final visit before departing forever to the grim underworld of shadows and the dead. She demanded he prove that his motives were pure and he suggested that they compete in bringing forth divine children. The one who produced red-blooded male offspring, he said, would be shown to be in the right.

Amaterasu took Susano's mighty sword, and she handed him the *magatama* or string of beads she wore in her hair. Piously they washed the blade and the jewels in the Ameno-mana, the deep heavenly well. Then Amaterasu bit into the sword,

39

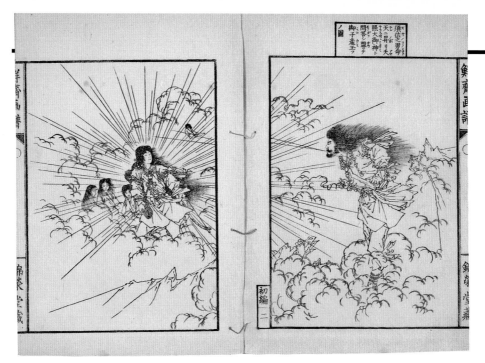

A 19th-century print illustrates the cosmic confrontation between the two elemental forces represented by Amaterasu and Susano. Here, Amaterasu stands alongside some of her handmaidens with whom she worked in the heavenly weaving hall, creating the divinities' garments – or even the very fabric of the universe itself.

crunching it in her strong jaws, and breathed out a bright mist that gave issue to three lithe goddesses. Susano chewed the beads and blew forth a cloudy breath that condensed into five strong gods.

The quintet of deities produced by Susano from Amaterasu's jewels were destined for a glorious future as guardians of the celestial realm, while the trio of goddesses that Amaterasu made from her brother's sword were dispatched to watch over the land of Japan in the Central Reed Plain. Between them, the eight children would in later ages be revered as ancestors of Jimmu, Japan's legendary first emperor, and of Japan's leading families.

Susano was not slow to point out that his triumph had proved his motives to be pure in the eyes of all Heaven. But Amaterasu quarrelled with him, saying that since the gods had come from her beads, she was in truth the victor in the contest.

Susano's wild nature drove him to a violent campaign of vengeance. Chaos swept at his heels through Heaven like a great thunderstorm punishing a country plain. He burst into the celestial rice fields, stamping on the soil and ruining the irrigation ditches and waters. Then, in the hall where the inhabitants of the celestial plain gathered each autumn to celebrate the harvest, he defecated and smeared his foul-smelling excrement.

Susano Attacks the Weaving Hall

According to some accounts, Amaterasu remained calm in the face of Susano's provocations and even made apologies for her brother to the other deities. But his next act was an outrage beyond excuse. He attacked the heavenly weaving hall in which Amaterasu and her maidens were at work.

It was part of the goddess's function to provide splendid garments for the deities of Heaven, and she had many female attendants to help her in this task. According to some accounts, the weaving maidens also made the clothes that were worn on Earth by priestesses of the imperial sun cult; other scholars suggest that their creation was the universe itself, which expanded little by little as they laboured at their looms.

On this day the workers were rudely interrupted in their sacred task by wild Susano, who captured and tortured a pony, tearing its bright and dappled skin from its back and hurling it into the hall (some scholars believe that the pony's dapples refer to the stars). One of Amaterasu's loyal servants died in the assault, for she was so frightened that she started forwards, injuring herself fatally on the shuttle of the loom at which she laboured. A terrified Amaterasu fled from the hall and hid herself in a cave known as Ama-no-Iwato ("Heavenly Rock Cave").

A Wondrous and Fulsome Harvest

Amaterasu, the great goddess of the sun, sent her brother Tsukiyomi, the god of the moon, to pay court to the food goddess Ogetsuno. Their divine encounter led to violence, but was not without a productive outcome.

Ogetsuno lived in the Central Reed Plain, where mortal men and women would one day settle, and Tsukiyomi descended from Heaven to visit her. Seeing the approach of so august a visitor, the goddess produced foods with which to welcome and entertain him.

When she pointed her head towards the land she gave issue to rice, while on setting her face towards the waters of the ocean she produced the many fish and other sea creatures. She faced the forbidding, snow-capped mountains and all the many creatures of the land, soft of pelt or covered with hard bristles, issued from her bodily orifices.

Tsukiyomi was disgusted that she was offering him food from her own body, and he drew his sword in anger. With a single stroke of the blade he brought the goddess down and returned to Heaven buzzing with satisfied anger. But the great Amaterasu was displeased when he spoke of his adventure and from that day forwards, the sun and moon were rarely seen together.

Amaterasu then sent another celestial deity, Amekumabito ("Heaven-bear-man"), to see the food goddess; scholars believe he may have been meant to represent a cloud, for clouds were often divine messengers in Japanese tradition. He found that

the food goddess was indeed dead, but from her body, like a fertile field supporting crops, came a wondrous harvest of good things. On her forehead grew millet; on her stomach,

rice; in her genitals wheat and beans; in her eyebrows were silkworms; while circling her head were the ancestors of those hardy animals of the field, the ox and the horse.

The Return of the Sun

With Amaterasu gone, darkness fell across Heaven and upon Japan below. Life abandoned a soil deprived of the sun's warm rays, and the crops failed; day and night were as one. The "800 myriads of gods" saw the need to restore order and they gathered on the banks of the heavenly river to seek a way of enticing the sun goddess out of her hideout.

The gods appealed to Omohi-kane, celebrated for his practical wisdom. On his advice they collected some cockerels, the sun goddess's sacred birds which – in normal times – herald her new coming each dawn. They then petitioned Tamahoya to make a great string of jewels, and Ishikori-dome to fashion a splendid, eight-sided mirror.

Next they brought a holy sakaki tree that had grown to maturity in rarified air on the high shoulder of a mountain and placed it near the cave in which Amaterasu had taken refuge. From its branches they hung the mirror clear as sky, the glittering jewels and long strands of coloured cloth. Several deities gathered round; they performed devotions and sacred rituals. Then Ameno Tajikarawo, who was known for his great physical strength, concealed himself close by the entrance to the rock cave.

The dawn goddess Ama-no-Uzume came forwards, clad in scanty clothing made from plants and streamers. She overturned a small tub and placed it opposite the cave door, next to the sacred sakaki tree. She lit holy fires, then, according to some versions, spoke a propitious incantation. The mirror, the strands of cloth that adorned the tree and the fires that the goddess lit were all later reproduced in Shinto shrines.

Ama-no-Uzume climbed onto the tub and began a lewd dance, as if her task was to seduce a haughty warrior or priest. Slowly she ground her hips and rolled her sleek belly, stamping her feet on the resonant tub. The assembled gods looked on with delight. She caught at her clothing, revealing her breasts, and then ripped away her undergarments, exposing herself completely. To the gods, indecency seemed a comic matter and they shouted with hearty laughter, so loud that Heaven shook as if it would turn itself inside out. At the same time the cockerels that the gods had gathered crowed mightily.

Amaterasu emerges from her cave, Ama-no-Iwato in southern Honshu, and restores sunshine to the world. The story perhaps has its origins in an ancient eclipse. Triptych, 19th century.

The Reflections of Perfection

Mirrors are common at Shinto shrines, constituting one of the religion's three main emblems alongside a necklace and a sword. By venerable tradition the mirror used to tempt Amaterasu out of the rock cave is the very one that is worshipped in the goddess's primary temple at Ise in Mie Prefecture.

The clearness of a mirror's surface and the sharpness of its reflections represent an ideal for worshippers, who are encouraged to clear distorting clouds of passion from their minds and hearts so that they present untroubled images of their souls to the deity.

The *Kojiki* recounts how Izanagi himself gave a mirror to his divine children and instructed them to view themselves in it morning and night; if they fixed their minds on the celestial and pure while driving out wickedness he said they would see a pure consciousness reflected.

A mirror was often said to hold the very soul of its owner. In one celebrated story a dying mother left a mirror to the daughter who had nursed her through a long illness that destroyed her good looks. The mirror was a marital gift from the dead mother's husband – the girl's father – and the faithful daughter was later comforted by the mirror's reflection, in which she believed she saw her mother with her youth and beauty restored.

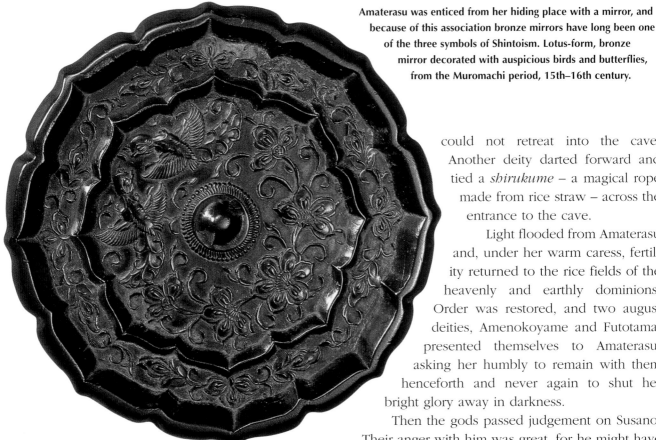

Amaterasu was enticed from her hiding place with a mirror, and because of this association bronze mirrors have long been one of the three symbols of Shintoism. Lotus-form, bronze mirror decorated with auspicious birds and butterflies, from the Muromachi period, 15th–16th century.

could not retreat into the cave. Another deity darted forward and tied a *shirukume* – a magical rope made from rice straw – across the entrance to the cave.

Light flooded from Amaterasu and, under her warm caress, fertility returned to the rice fields of the heavenly and earthly dominions. Order was restored, and two august deities, Amenokoyame and Futotama, presented themselves to Amaterasu, asking her humbly to remain with them henceforth and never again to shut her bright glory away in darkness.

Then the gods passed judgement on Susano. Their anger with him was great, for he might have caused a disaster in Heaven and on Earth. They fined him heavily, ordered his beard to be shaved and the nails to be cut from his hands and feet. They made him recite propitious phrases used in purification rituals and make offerings of his mucus and spittle. Finally, the gods barred Susano forever from Heaven and, warning him not to rest on Earth, then dispatched him to the dark and unwelcoming underworld.

Order and Chaos

Some scholars read the episode of Amaterasu's disappearance as a mythological account of a solar eclipse, while others – pointing to Susano's desecration of the hall used for the autumn festival – see it as a myth of winter and returning spring. In many cultures sexual licence and impropriety are associated with agricultural fertility rites; Ama-no-Uzume's lewd dance may be part of a rite intended to lure the sun back from winter exile.

Deep within her cave refuge, Amaterasu heard the cockerels and felt the vibration caused by the gods' laughter. She could not understand what could have provoked such rejoicing, for she knew that without her brightness the wide expanses of both Heaven and Earth would be submerged in gloom and deprived of fertility. She opened the door to listen, then called out, asking what was the cause of such a commotion. Ama-no-Uzume answered craftily that the gods were rejoicing for they had found a mistress better than Amaterasu. Then curiosity proved too much for the sun goddess. She looked out and saw the mirror that the gods had hung in the sakaki tree and, captivated by its bright image, came further forwards – looking intently at the reflection of her own great glory, which she had never seen before.

In that instant the mighty Ameno Tajikarawo leaped forward and caught her hand so that she

Ama-no-Uzume who coaxed the sun to reappear may well have been imported with Buddhism. Some writers identify her as a distant relation of the dawn goddess of Indo-European myth, who became Eos in Greek tradition and was lyrically celebrated as Usas in the Aryan Indian scripture the *Rig Veda* (*c*.1000BC).

The divine quarrel between Amaterasu and Susano also represents a clash, familiar from other mythological and religious traditions, between universal order in the form of the great sun goddess and the force of chaos – Susano, unruly as a whirlwind or a thunderstorm. The Japanese myths were first collected in the *Kojiki* to glorify the emperor, and in this context the triumph of Amaterasu may be meant to symbolize the glory of lawfulness and sound government established by the imperial dynasty in ancient times.

The Romantic Star Festival of Tanabata

There are few stories about stars in Japanese mythology. One tale – which was imported from China, where it was known as "The Cowherd and the Girl Weaver" – concerns the creation of the Milky Way and is celebrated in the festival of Tanabata held every year on 7 July.

This romantic tale concerns a brawny herdsman who fell in love with a beautiful girl weaver of delicate artistry. The weaver was a goddess – in the Chinese original her grandmother was the great divinity Xi Wang Mu. In the Japanese version the weaver's father was the God of the Sky, who was displeased by her dalliance and whisked her off to the heavenly realm. Her devoted herdsman followed; then the father created the great celestial river of the Milky Way to keep the herdsman at bay. But the young man's devotion was such that in the end the god relented and allowed the two lovers to cross the river once a year – on the seventh day of the seventh month – over a bridge formed by magpies. Then they dwell in each other's loving company for one short summer night.

The girl weaver was called Tanabata and was associated with the constellation known to the Japanese by that name – and to Westerners as Vega in the constellation Lyra. On the night of Tanabata, the women and girls who primarily celebrate this festival of romantic love suspend paper streamers and twisted wool or cotton threads from tree branches. On the papers they have devotedly written poems about the celestial lovers or petitions for their own success in affairs of the heart. They also pour out water in a shallow dish and observe the reflection of the stars in the water; then they cast leaves of the kaji tree into the bowl, seeking in the movements of the water and of the leaves a divine signal as to their own chances in love.

Tanabata is explained to a young girl in this 18th-century print by Utamaro.

A Myriad of Deities

Many of the multitudinous Shinto gods do not play an active role in Japanese creation mythology and the celestial struggle between Amaterasu and Susano. Instead, they represent the everyday elements, aspects of nature or human behaviour.

The Sacred High Ground

When a furious Izanagi dispatched the fire god who had killed Izanami, he struck five clean blows with his sword, transforming him into five mountain deities. The first was Oyamazumi, chief of mountains, the second Nakayamazumi, the *kami* of the sheer mountain slopes. The other three were gods of parts of the mountain – one of the upper slopes, one of the lower slopes and one of the foothills. Mountains were ancient objects of reverence in Japan, and each sacred peak naturally enough was believed to have its own *kami*. Mount Fuji was pre-eminent but others included Mount Aso and Mount Nantai. There was also a god of rock called Oiwa Daimyojin.

Gods of Weather

On forbidding slopes among the mountain deities lived the rain god, Taka-Okami. Far below, where the land plunged into steep valleys thick with vegetation, Kura-Okami, controller of snow as well as rainstorms, was found. When rain was needed, worshippers made offerings to these deities. Another god, Takitsu-Hiko ("Cataract Prince"), lived in the form of a rock on Mount Kaminabi in Izumo and, if propitiated, would release rains into the skies when drought strangled the Earth.

Susano was associated with storms and thunder, but there were other thunder gods – notably Kaminari, who was worshipped in many Shinto shrines. A sword – symbolizing lightning – was hung in shrines to Kaminari as a *shintai*, the object into which the deity would enter during rites.

The wooded gorge at Sounkyo in Hokkaido has the powerful *kami* essence of the gods of both mountains and waterfalls.

Trees struck and split by lightning were traditionally not felled for timber because they had been chosen by the god. According to seventh-century annals, an official who ignored this taboo and ordered the cutting down of a tree that had been torn asunder provoked the ire of Kaminari. The god unleashed a violent thunderstorm which went crashing over the forest in which the tree stood, sending the official running for his life.

Water and Wind

Each great river had its own *kami*, and even springs and wells had their own living invisible divinities attached to them. The god of wells was Mii who gives or withholds the waters of the Earth. Izanagi created many sea gods during the bath in which he purified himself after his descent to the underworld (see page 31); while the governing deity of the waters was called Watazumi.

Shinatsu, god of sweet winds, sprang from the mouth of Izanagi when he desired to clear the mists that clung to the fair land of Japan each morning. His paramour was the goddess Shinatobe of fragrant breath. Tatsuta and his goddess Tasuta were also wind deities, propitiated with great devotion by fisherman and sailors – for the divine controllers of the winds, when roused, could bring a fleet to swift ruin. Violent and widely feared was Hayatsumuji, the god of the spinning whirlwind.

A Divine Land

On a more solid plane, even the roads had gods with the power to prevent misfortune befalling their devotees. Theirs was a phallic cult; their *shintai* was a stick planted in the ground. The road gods had no fixed sanctuaries but were worshipped twice a year at crossroads or town entrances. Some scholars believe that before the coming of Buddhism in the sixth-century AD stone phalluses were traditionally raised at crossroads, and there is also evidence that a phallus would be put up in a rice field in the belief that it would keep away pests. Chimata was celebrated as deity of crossroads and Yachimata and Yachimatao as god and goddess of roads beyond number; Kunado was god of the place that should not be visited and Funado of the place that must not be violated.

In the countryside the fields had their own goddess, Nuzuchi, who was also known as the Princess of the Grass. There was a deity to protect leaves and one resident in tree trunks. The rice god was Inari, imagined as an old man who sat habitually on a sack of rice flanked by two sleek, bushy tailed foxes – his messengers. Sometimes, however, Inari was seen as a goddess of delicate beauty and lithe movements, on occasion linked to the goddess of agriculture, Uganomitama, and at other times to the beautiful Indian goddess of prosperity, Lakshmi. Inari was particularly worshipped during a spring festival held to mark the sowing of rice. She or he was revered also as the patron deity of swordsmiths and was widely worshipped as a divinity of prosperity and trade, possessing the power to give or withhold wealth.

Guardians of Fortune

Highly reminiscent of China's Eight Immortals, the Shichi Fukujin, "Seven Gods of Luck" (or "Happiness"), were widely celebrated and revered. Serene Hotei, whose big belly protruded from his loose garments, was essentially a Buddhist figure. He was renowned for his

The Seven Gods of Luck – one is actually a goddess – were best known for their journey in a treasure ship. Four of the pantheon are visible in this late 19th-century ivory netsuke.

generosity and willingness to perform good deeds such as carrying women travellers across rivers. He carried a fan and hoisted a great bag on his back.

Elderly Jurojin carried a scroll on which was recorded all the world's most precious wisdom. He travelled in the company of a tortoise, a crane and a stag – all symbols of a contented and satisfied old age. Because of his great age he was tradition-ally shown leaning on a staff.

Fukurokuju, with a tiny body and a great elongated head, brought wisdom and long-lasting good fortune. By tradition he was once a philoso-pher in China. Bishamon, another Buddhist-influ-enced figure (as guardian of the north – see page 33), appeared clad in armour, clasping in one hand a tiny pagoda and in the other a great spear.

Daikoku, god of wealth, sat on bales of rice clasping a magical hammer said to have the power to grant petitions brought forward in pure devo-tion. Rats stole his rice but he remained serene.

Ebisu was celebrated as god of hard work, particularly of labouring fishermen and traders. Images show him bearing a fishing rod and hold-ing a fish – usually tai, or bream – newly plucked from the teeming waters. The goddess Benten was also traditionally linked with the sea and the arts. Shrines in her honour were built on islands or near the mainland shore. In images she was depicted with a dragon or sea serpent.

The seven play a major role in Japan's tradi-tional New Year Eve festivities, when, according to folklore, the *Takara Bune*, or phantom treasure ship, bearing them sails into harbour each year. The gods bring a cargo of precious things (*takara-mono*) such as a bottomless purse, a holy key and a coat of good fortune. Images of the ship are sold on New Year's Eve and believers who buy one put it in a bedside drawer in the conviction that it will bring them good luck through their dreams.

Where Shinto Meets Buddhism

The Seven Gods of Luck offer a good example of a very Japanese fusion of religious influences, for scholars believe the Shichi Fukujin may have had no place in ancient Shinto. They appear to have existed in their present form only since c.1600 and elements of Hinduism, Buddhism and Chinese Daoism combine with Shinto in these deities. Daikoku and Ebisu are probably the only ones to derive from Shinto tradition.

Far earlier than this – in the eighth century – Ryobu Shinto, in which Shinto deities were associ-ated with Buddhas and bodhisattvas (see box opposite), developed. Its creation is usually cred-ited to the monk Kobo Daishi (774–834). In this era Amaterasu came to be identified with the eter-nal or cosmic Buddha Dainichi Nyorai or Vairocana and the Shinto war god Hachiman was matched to the bodhisattva Dai Bosatsu.

Gods in History

A number of historical or semi-legendary figures of Japanese history rose after their death to become gods in the Shinto pantheon. Most celebrated of these was the great warrior leader Emperor Ojin who died c.AD394 (see pages 86–87). In the early eighth century Empress Gemmyo built a shrine to him at Usa and he became the god of war, Hachiman. In modern times there are many shrines in his honour, where young men hold coming-of-age ceremonies to mark their entry into adulthood at the age of twenty. Believers venerate pigeons as the messengers of Hachiman.

Another Shinto god was once a scholar by the name of Sugawara Michizane (845–903) who had to end his life in exile in Kyushu after his enemies misrepresented him to to the emperor. By tradition his favourite tree was the plum, and an often-told legend recounts how a plum tree lifted its roots and was carried on a fragrant breeze from his abandoned garden in Kyoto to his place of exile. He became the Shinto god of learning and callig-raphy, Tenjin, patron deity of scholars. Because he was said to use a bull as a means of transport, there are often images of bulls in his shrines.

Shinto has continued to create new gods and in the twentieth century Emperor Meiji, who died in 1912, was elevated to the Shinto pantheon.

The Enlightened Beings

The Japanese practised the Mahayana ("Greater Vehicle") form of Buddhism in which bodhisattvas, or bosatsus in Japanese – beings who delay entry into nirvana and incarnate on Earth in order to help humans towards the goal of release from the cycle of birth and death – came to be revered as deities.

The bodhisattva Kannon Bosatsu was believed to be of infinite mercy and compassion – the Japanese version of Avalokitesvara in Indian tradition. Kannon was a manifestation or disciple of Amida Buddha, the protector of humankind and guardian of the western paradise (see page 33). He was represented in many different ways, the three principal ones being: Sho Kannon, serene of face and wearing jewels like a earthly prince; Senju Kannon, with 1,000 arms; and the eleven-headed Ju-ichimen Kannon.

Bodhisattvas were beyond sexual difference; many Japanese images of Kannon give him a feminine aspect but none actually represents him as a woman. The cult of Kannon dated from Japanese Buddhism's early years; a bronze statue of Kannon in Horyuji monastery is from 651.

The bodhisattva Jizo Bosatsu was revered as protector of suffering humans – particularly of children, pregnant women and travellers. In Japanese Buddhism the souls of the dead were believed to pass to hell for judgement and punishment; Jizo, full of pity, was worshipped as friend and adviser of the dead at

Edo-period wooden bodhisattva atop a white lotus pedestal; this floral imagery is often associated with Mount Fuji.

their judgement, when he used his great accumulated goodness to win sinners a reprieve from at least part of the dreadful fate they had earned.

Deep among the shadows of hell was a riverbank named Sainokawara, where children who had died young and whose parents had failed to pray for their rebirth built shrines from the pebbles on the beach. Jizo protected and comforted these poor young ones like a father or mother. Statues of Jizo often show him in a child's apron and have pebbles piled at the feet.

Another important bodhisattva was Monju Bosatsu – known elsewhere as Manjusri – an incarnation of the wisdom beyond compare that comes with enlightenment. He was usually shown astride a lion, holding a sword and a scroll.

Fugen Bosatsu – or Samantabhadra – was revered for wisdom and compassionate understanding of human error. Typically he was depicted sitting on a lotus flower supported by a six-tusked white elephant. According to legend, Fugen took the form of a courtesan to appear to the monk Shoku (910–1007), demonstrating that the Buddha's wise nature was found even in the worst of sinners.

SUMO: A DIVINE CONTEST

According to the *Kojiki*, the supremacy of the Japanese people on the islands of Japan was supposedly established when the god Takamimusubi won a brutal bout of wrestling against Take-minakata, representing a rival clan. Whatever its origins, sumo is a very ancient sport dating back some 1,500 years. Early matches were highly ritualized affairs dedicated to the gods, with prayers for a bountiful harvest combined with sacred dancing and dramas within the precincts of shrines. Today too, the most remarkable aspect of the modern sport is its adherence to ritual and ceremony. Pre-fight observances, partly drawn from the battlefield, demonstrate sumo's Shinto origins and intensify the psychological tension in the arena. The stamping and slapping is thought to be derived from some of the divine actions undertaken to lure Amaterasu from her cave (see page 42).

Left: Hotei and Daikoku, gods of generosity and wealth respectively, depicted as sumo wrestlers. Ivory netsuke, early 19th century.

Below: Although the history of sumo dates back more than 1,000 years, it has been organized in professional tournaments only since the 18th century. *Rikishi* or wrestlers are promoted purely on the basis of merit according to their performances in bouts. Here two *rikishi* are shown in a training bout within the confines of their own *heya* or stable. A 19th-century woodblock print from a triptych by Utagawa Kunisada.

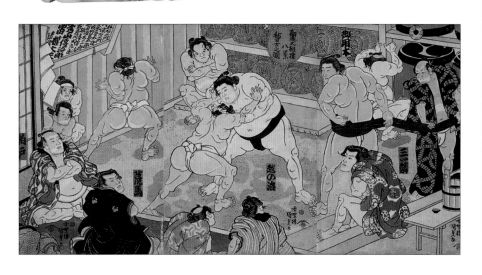

Left: Salt is thrown by the wrestler in order to cleanse the *dohyo* or ring and drive out evil spirits. Another pre-bout purification ritual involves pouring sake into the *dohyo.*

Below: Following the purification, the *rikishi* perform the *shikiri,* an elaborate series of rituals prior to the commencement of the bout. The *dohyo* is a three-dimensional clay construction with a ring marked out in *tawara* or straw bales. Just outside the circle the cardinal directions are marked by four *tokudawara.* It is only on these that the contestant can step outside the ring and not be deemed to have lost.

THE DIVINE DYNASTY

For centuries the Japanese believed that their emperor was different from other men, a god upon Earth. Not only was he divinely chosen – as many other peoples believed of their kings – but he was a member of a divine family, a direct descendant of the sun goddess Amaterasu herself. It was only in 1946, in the terrible aftermath of defeat in World War II, that the then emperor, Hirohito, renounced this divinity.

The emperor's divine status lies close to the heart of Japanese mythology. An important cycle of Japanese myths contained in the eighth-century *Kojiki* and *Nihongi* describes the exploits of Amaterasu's grandson and his descendants, culminating in the triumphs of Jimmu, Japan's legendary first emperor. It was the central purpose of the compilers of the *Kojiki* and *Nihongi* – which are scholars' principal sources for Japanese myth (see page 15) – to establish the imperial family's divine lineage and its right to rule as part of the sun goddess's eternally ordained plan for Japan.

Opposite: A 19th-century *surimono*, or privately issued print, from a series entitled *The Three Imperial Regalia*. The woman holds the sacred sword in her hand.

The celestial deities Izanagi and Izanami descended to Earth to create the lands of Japan, but they did not remain; Izanami's death banished her to the underworld of Yomi, while Izanagi, according to the principal version of this myth, withdrew once more to Heaven. The Earth was left in the hands of unruly myriads of lower deities. When chaotic Susano caused uproar in Heaven he was banished and – en route to the underworld – stopped on Earth in the Izumo region of western Japan, rescuing the beautiful Kusanada-hime (Rice Paddy Princess) from being devoured by a menacing, eight-headed giant serpent. A distinct cycle of myths set in the Izumo region, and known to scholars as the Izumo cycle, begins with Susano's descent from Heaven and continues with the exploits of his descendant Okuninushi, the "Great Lord of the Country".

Below: A mirror, made of bronze and adorned with chrysanthemums in a tortoiseshell pattern. The flower is Japan's imperial symbol. Muromachi period, 16th century.

In the reign of Okuninushi, conflict and lawlessness on Earth made Amaterasu decide to send down her representatives to impose control. Then she instructed her grandson, Honinigi, that his destiny was to establish a dynasty on Earth that would draw strength from its links to the heavenly divinities and would endure as long as Heaven and Earth themselves endured. Honinigi's great-grandson was Jimmu; Emperor Hirohito, who died in 1989, was believed to be the 124th ruler of Japan descended in a direct line from Jimmu.

53

Susano in Exile

Susano, driven out of Heaven, descended to the Izumo region in western Honshu. There he paused next to a river, seeking to calm his troubled soul. When he saw chopsticks floating in the water he guessed that there must be people living nearby and set off upstream to find them.

Before long he came upon an odd grouping – a young woman of radiant beauty and an elderly couple. All three were crying, railing loudly against fate, then moaning low with grief. Susano asked what was the matter. The old man revealed himself to be of divine lineage – a grandson of Izanagi and Izanami (and therefore Susano's nephew). His name was Ashinadzuchi ("Foot-stroke-elder") and his wife was Tenadzuchi ("Hand-stroke-elder").

The husband and wife explained that they had once rejoiced in eight delicate daughters, but one evil day Yamata no Orochi, a huge snake with eight heads and eight tails, had come from the Koshi district to prey upon them. Each year it returned and ate one of their daughters, until now only the youngest, Kusanada-hime ("Rice Paddy Princess"), remained. Before the day was out the snake would arrive and dispatch their daughter, leaving them without a comforter in their old age.

The princess's beauty made Susano quicken with desire and he respectfully told the elderly couple that as brother of the great sun goddess he too was of divine lineage, and thus a relation. Then he calmly offered to kill the serpent in return for their daughter's hand in marriage. The princess's parents were quick to agree and broad-chested Susano swept her up, transformed her into a hair comb and hid her safely in his long locks.

Susano slays the eight-headed serpent Yamata no Orochi, shown here by the artist as an unpacified dragon coming up out of a raging sea. Hanging scroll by Kawanabe Kyosai, 1887.

The Divine Origin of Charms

There is a Japanese custom of charms and talismans, or omamori. Some are worn, while others are pinned up on the gateway of a house to offer protection against contagions. One explanation for this protective practice attributes Susano with power over disease and foul plagues.

The tale recounts how one stormy night Susano wandered across the lands of the Central Reed Plain, his poor clothing offering him scant protection from the elements. At the house of Kotan-Shorai, Susano knocked and asked for shelter. But Kotan-Shorai was unimpressed by the stranger's scruffiness and refused to grant him entry.

Then Susano went to a nearby house, that of Somin-Shorai, Kotan-Shorai's brother. Opening his door Somin saw a sad traveller with the wind howling at his back and at once asked him in. He fed his guest and gave him sake to warm him, then showed him into a sleeping area to rest. The next morning, when Susano came to leave, he

revealed his true identity and pledged that to the end of time Somin and his descendants would be free of the wicked spirits that cause disease, as long as they hung a sign at their gatepost to ward off the spirits. And since that day the Japanese have displayed notices on their gateposts identifying them as descendants of Somin-Shorai.

He asked the parents to bring him a great draught of sake rice wine. This he poured into eight deep bowls, which he laid out to tempt the snake. Then they all concealed themselves close by and waited.

Susano Slays the Snake

When Yamata no Orochi appeared, the parents shivered with fright. The beast was as long as eight great hills divided by eight plunging valleys; its red eyes glowered and along its back grew cypress trees and tall firs. It lowered its eight heads to the bowls of sake and drank greedily. Soon its long eight-tailed body lost its strength and it slumped into a drunken stupor. Then Susano stood tall, drew his long sword and sliced the beast into eighty pieces.

As Susano chopped at one of its middle tails he struck hard metal. When he investigated he discovered a great sword hidden in the flesh. It was a weapon fit for a goddess and Susano afterwards delivered Murakumo ("Assembled Clouds") to his sister Amaterasu as a gift. This sword became a symbol of the imperial clan's rule and, renamed Kusanagi ("Mower of Grass"), was later used to heroic effect by Yamato-takeru (see pages 78–79).

The princess's parents rejoiced with Susano as he drew the comb from his hair, restoring the maiden to human shape. Then at Suga, in Izumo, he raised a great palace with eight tall walls and took up residence with his new wife and her parents. There they lived a blessed life. Fittingly for a deity associated with fertility he was father to many children, one of whom, Okuninushi, became the hero of a myth cycle (see pages 56–61).

Susano the Hirsute Creator

In another version of this myth, Susano made trees for Japan by plucking the hairs from his virile body – an aspect some have suggested links him to the Ainu, the more hirsute aboriginal Japanese. Susano made cryptomeria trees from chin bristles; thuyas, a kind of pine, using chest hairs; camphor trees from eyebrow hairs; and podocarpus, or maki, another pine, from buttock hairs. He decreed that the peoples of Japan should build boats from the wood of camphor and cryptomeria in order to trade and create wealth, while with thuya they should raise Shinto shrines across the landscape. Podocarpus timber was set aside for making coffins in which to lay the dead to rest.

The Trials of Okuninushi

The beauty and feminine grace of Princess Yagami-hime of Inaba was famed far and wide, and the many sons of Kusanada-hime and great Susano resolved to travel to her country and compete for her hand in marriage. They voyaged in a large group, eighty in number, with their young brother Okuninushi coming behind, in charge of their baggage.

At Cape Keta the eighty brothers encountered a poor furless rabbit by the roadside. The brothers stopped to examine the pitiful creature and cruelly misadvised it, suggesting that it bathe in salt water and then dry out in the wind. They knew that this would make its skin crack painfully, but the unsuspecting rabbit did as they advised.

When Okuninushi came by the creature was in terrible agony, its skin badly split by the chill wind. He asked the rabbit how it came to its sad plight. The rabbit told him that it had been stuck on the island of Oki with no way of crossing the waters to the mainland when it met a group of crocodiles and tricked them into helping it across.

First it engaged them in a jesting conversation about whether the rabbit's relatives or the crocodiles were greater in number, then proposed a way of finding out the answer: if the crocodiles lay together across the strait to create a link with the cape, the rabbit would skip lightly across, counting them as it went. The crocodiles agreed, and the rabbit made the crossing. But foolishly, just before it reached the mainland, it taunted them by revealing that it was not counting their number at all and had only tricked them into providing a bridge. At

A fierce crocodile thrashing violently in Japanese waters. Colour woodblock print by Kuniyoshi, c.1849.

this the final crocodile flew into a rage and seized the rabbit in its strong jaws. In its effort to escape, the animal had lost its fur.

So, the rabbit went on, it had been lying shivering by the roadside when the eighty deities came by and advised it to bathe in salt water. Upset by their malice, Okuninushi used his detailed knowledge of natural medicine and magical rites to help. He told the rabbit to travel to the river's mouth and wash in the soft waters, then to sprinkle the pollen from the kama grass that grew on the bank and to roll in it. The rabbit did as it was told and its fur was restored.

Then the rabbit, who was in truth an animal deity, declared to Okuninushi that it knew the eighty deities were his brothers and that they all travelled in search of the hand in marriage of fair Princess Yagami-hime of Inaba. It revealed that none of the brothers would be successful, for the princess would marry Okuninushi himself.

(One aspect of Okuninushi is as a healer; some scholars identify him as a patron of ancient Japanese shamans and suggest that the purpose of the rabbit deity tale is to establish Okuninushi's great healing powers. The story of the marital quest and the Izumo prince Okuninushi's success in it can be explained as a myth about the conquest of Inaba by the rulers of Izumo; this may have been achieved partly through intermarriage.)

At the very time that Okuninushi was helping the poor rabbit, his eighty brothers were in audience with Princess Yagami-hine. She revealed that she would not take any of them, for she had set her heart on Okuninushi. And when in due course he arrived, the couple were married.

Revenge of the Spurned Brothers

Rejection drove the brothers to cold fury and they plotted how they could do away with the precocious Okuninushi. At Mount Tema they asked him to help capture a wild red boar that lived on the peak. They would climb the sheer mountain slopes and drive the animal down. His task was to catch it and tie it up.

Then the brothers went stealthily away and heated a great boulder. They sent it crashing down the mountainside – and Okuninushi, mistaking it for the boar, tried to catch it and was burned to death. The brothers' enjoyment of their revenge was short-lived, for their mother, Kusanada-hime, climbed to Heaven and petitioned the great deity Kamimusubi (see page 32) to restore Okuninushi to life. The deity sent two celestial princesses who bathed Okuninushi's burned body with a magical soothing potion; and he was transformed once more into a young man of beauty and strength.

Okuninushi's brothers followed him, biding their time. Before long they had killed him a second time, crushing him in the fork of a split mountain tree. Then Kusanada-hime found him, took him tenderly from the tree and caressed him until he was alive again. She counselled him to flee from his brothers to the underground realm of his father, Susano, for she saw that they would not rest until they had done away with him.

He followed her advice at once but even then he was pursued by the eighty deities who would have killed him again with their arrows had he he not slipped magically through the fork in a tree where they could not follow.

The Tests of Susano

Okuninushi travelled fearlessly into the shadowy underworld until he found Susano's dwelling. In that place he encountered a young woman of great beauty, who was Susano's daughter Suseri-hime. He gazed at her and she looked upon his bright features, and love touched them both. Without delay they married, even in that dark

Having evaded his brothers' arrows, Okuninushi was to obtain a bow and arrows himself with which to humble his jealous siblings.

57

place. They were both children of Susano and therefore brother and sister, but like Izanagi and Izanami and many other divine siblings in Japanese mythology, they also became husband and wife.

Susano was displeased, but he pretended to welcome Okuninushi so that he might test his mettle. The first night he put his guest in a room of snakes, but Suseri-hime gave Okuninushi a scarf with the power to drive them back. On the second night, Okuninushi had to contend with centipedes and bees, but again he was equipped with a magical scarf provided by his wife. For a third test Susano took an arrow and fired it far away into a wide plain, bidding Okuninushi go and retrieve it.

Susano waited a while, then set fire to the plain's tall grasses and sent a stiff breeze to fan the flames. Okuninushi saw the blaze raging towards him from all directions and looked around for a way out, but he had travelled too far and there was no escape. Calmly he prepared for death, but then a field mouse approached him and told him a

riddle: "The inside is hollow, the outside narrow." By this it meant that nearby there was an underground cave where Okuninushi could shelter from the flames. Okuninushi worked out the riddle, found the small entrance and was saved.

After the blaze had passed, the mouse brought Okuninushi the arrow that Susano had fired into the plain. Okuninushi took the prize back and presented it to Susano. Some time afterwards Okuninushi was waiting on the great storm god, combing his hair and picking out the creatures that he found crawling on the scalp. Soothed, Susano fell asleep and Okuninushi saw his chance. He tied Susano's hair to the rafters and took his host's sword, bow and lyre. Then he sealed the palace by rolling a boulder across its entrance.

Okuninushi literally swept Suseri-hime off her feet, put her over his shoulder and set off at a run.

Tales of Izumo

According to Izumo tradition, it was Okuninushi and a mysterious dwarf god called Sukunabiko – rather than Izanagi and Izanami – who created the islands of Japan.

Returning from the underworld (see main text), Okuninushi rested at Cape Mipo in Izumo. On the restless sea he saw a diminutive god adrift in a boat made from the tiny pod of a kagami plant. Okuninushi addressed himself to the newcomer, asking his name – but received no reply. Then he asked the god's many attendants, but they too remained silent. At that the toad – a great traveller and therefore knowledgeable

about many arcane things – spoke up, suggesting that Okuninushi speak to Kuyebiko, the scarecrow, about the matter.

Kuyebiko, summoned into Okuninushi's presence, said that the dwarf god was named Sukunabiko and was the son of the great goddess Kamimusubi. Then Okuninushi inquired of Kamimusubi as to whether this was true and she declared that it was so, and proclaimed that it was the task reserved for

In their haste they knocked against a branch and the lyre released a sweet, invigorating chord that woke Susano. He guessed at once what was afoot but he could not give chase straightaway because he first had to untie his hair. By the time he came near to Okuninushi and Suseri-hime they had already passed the boundary between the underworld and the Central Land of the Reed Plain above. He could see them labouring up the slope ahead of him towards the brightness of the fields, and he called out a generous farewell, advising Okuninushi to use the bow and sword to humble his unruly brothers. Then he should become ruler of the land and settle near Mount Uka, making Suseri-hime his senior wife.

It all came to pass as Susano had foretold. Okuninushi defeated his brothers, who accepted his overlordship and settled in the area near Mount Uka, which was important in the Izumo region and was where men later built the Great Shrine of Izumo – the second most sacred of all Shinto shrines in Japan, after that of Amaterasu at Ise.

According to the Izumo myth cycle, after his sojourn in the underworld Okuninushi and a deity named Sukunabiko created the land of Japan (see box below) – a task attributed elsewhere to Izanagi and Izanami. Some scholars suggest that Okuninushi finished the work done by Izanagi and Izanami. Others argue that there were two distinct creation myths – one, featuring Okuninushi, from the Izumo region, and another featuring Izanagi and Izanami, from the Yamato region. Although the *Kojiki* was a Yamato project, the Izumo creation myth still survived.

Okuninushi lived with Suseri-hime and his first wife Yagami-hime, but Yagami-hime grew unhappy, for she was afraid of Suseri-hime, and she abandoned her place in Okuninushi's bed, returning to her parents' house.

Okuninushi and Sukunabiko to give form to the islands of the Central Land of the Reed Plain.

After the two gods had performed this honourable task, Sukunabiko travelled on in his tiny craft to Tokoyo-no-Kuni, the distant land of eternity beyond the ocean.

Okuninushi spoke aloud in grief demanding to know how he alone could keep order in the land. Then a mysterious deity appeared like a band of heavenly light across the ocean and agreed to help him govern Japan. He declared that he would always be at Okuninushi's side if he would in return establish a shrine for the god's worship on the sacred peak of Mount Mimoro.

A later ruler of Izumo was Omitsunu ("Master Field Beach"), a grandson of Susano. He enlarged Izumo territory in a novel way.

Omitsunu was troubled that Izumo was so small and he saw that across the water there was spare land lying untended on the shore of Korea. Therefore he took a rope, tied one end to the Korean shore and the other to a peak in Izumo, Mount Sahime, and ordered his subjects to pull for their lives. A great mass of land tore away and attached itself to Izumo. He later repeated the trick, using ropes to haul in islands from the Sea of Japan and mould them on to Izumo. The remains of the last rope made the beach of Yomi.

The Battle for the Reed Plain

Following his struggles with Susano, Okuninushi had to contend with the great sun goddess Amaterasu, who wished to enlarge her celestial kingdom to encompass the territory occupied by men and women in the Central Land of the Reed Plain.

The gods in the celestial realm were only too aware of the strife among the inhabitants of the Central Land of the Reed Plain. In this era, according to one myth, the plants, rocks and trees of Japan could speak and regularly disturbed the calm of night by sending complaints up to Heaven.

Amaterasu dispatched Ama-no-ho, one of the sons born of her contest with Susano (see page 40), to investigate, but on arriving he forgot his mission and settled on Earth without sending word back. Then she sent Ama-no-ho's son, but he too failed to report. Next she sent a deity named Ame-no-waka-hiko, armed with a divine bow and arrow, who was famed for his fearlessness and prowess in battle. But even he proved unreliable: he seduced Okuninushi's daughter, Shitateru-hime, and settled in Izumo.

After eight more years of silence, Amaterasu next dispatched a divine pheasant to Earth to seek out Ame-no-waka-hiko. It alighted on a cassia tree near the god's dwelling and there it stayed, waiting for its chance to talk to Ame-no-waka-hiko. When one of the women of the house complained that it was an evil omen, Ame-no-waka-hiko drew one of his divine arrows and shot the pheasant. The projectile passed through the bird and winged its way directly to Heaven, where the deity Takamimusubi deflected it back to Earth – and it dealt Ame-no-waka-hiko a fatal wound as he slept.

Shitateru-hime was distraught at her husband's death and her wailing and cries of grief could be heard even in Heaven. The gods sent down a sweet wind that carried Ame-no-waka-hiko's body back to the divine realm. There they built a mortuary house, laid the body reverently in it and joined Shitateru-hime in her mourning. For eight days and nights they watched over the body, crying and lamenting the death. An earthly friend of Ame-no-waka-hiko by the name of Ajishiki went to console Shitateru-hime but because he looked so like the deceased, all the members of the household cried out and swarmed around him, declaring that he was in truth Ame-no-waka-hiko returned to life. Ajishiki was angered and with a great sword attacked the heavenly mortuary house in which his friend's body lay. It fell to Earth where it took the form of Mount Moyama.

The Goddess's Ultimatum

Now Amaterasu sent the deities Takamimusubi and Kamimusubi (see page 32) to inform Okuninushi that he must surrender his realm to her. In a gesture asserting sovereignty, the two divinities each took a glittering sword and sunk the handles into the crest of a breaking wave off Inasa beach in Izumo. Here, sitting cross-legged on the sword-tips, they materialized before Okuninushi. They informed him that the land of men and women was destined to be ruled by offspring of Amaterasu and demanded a swift response.

Okuninushi declined to answer, saying that his son Yakoto-shironushi would speak in his stead. The son was summoned and advised submitting to the illustrious deities. Some scholars believe that Yakoto-shironushi represented a priest or god of ritual language and for this reason he was the one summoned to communicate with the divine messengers.

Shortly afterwards another of Okuninushi's sons, the combative Take-minakata, appeared on the beach, balancing a great boulder on his finger-tips as a show of strength and demanding the chance to contest the decision with the deities. He

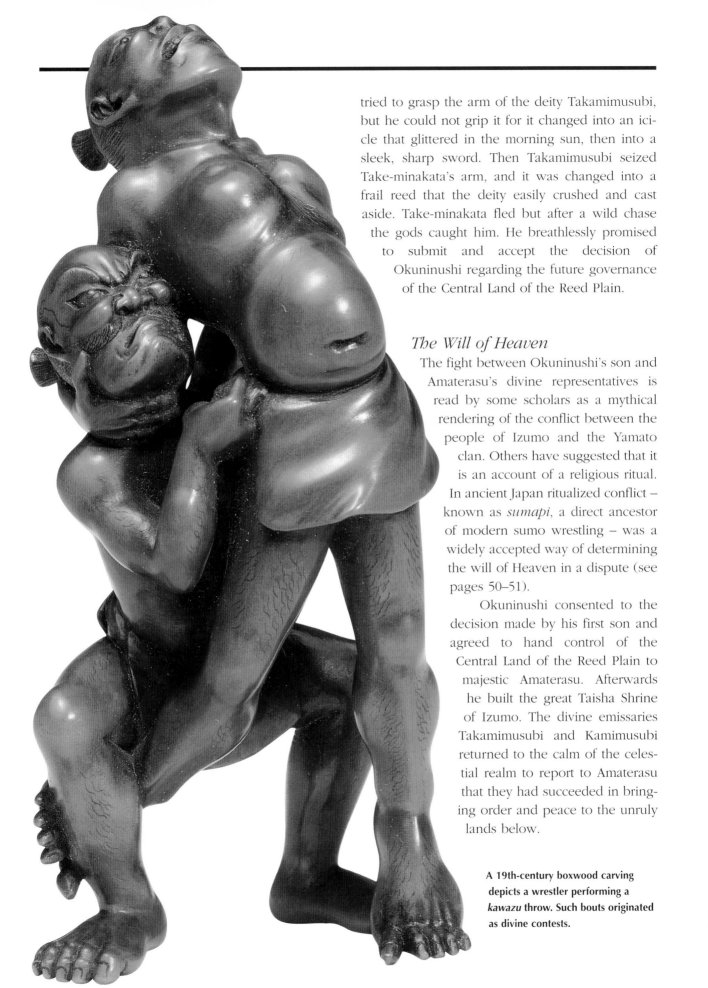

tried to grasp the arm of the deity Takamimusubi, but he could not grip it for it changed into an icicle that glittered in the morning sun, then into a sleek, sharp sword. Then Takamimusubi seized Take-minakata's arm, and it was changed into a frail reed that the deity easily crushed and cast aside. Take-minakata fled but after a wild chase the gods caught him. He breathlessly promised to submit and accept the decision of Okuninushi regarding the future governance of the Central Land of the Reed Plain.

The Will of Heaven

The fight between Okuninushi's son and Amaterasu's divine representatives is read by some scholars as a mythical rendering of the conflict between the people of Izumo and the Yamato clan. Others have suggested that it is an account of a religious ritual. In ancient Japan ritualized conflict – known as *sumapi*, a direct ancestor of modern sumo wrestling – was a widely accepted way of determining the will of Heaven in a dispute (see pages 50–51).

Okuninushi consented to the decision made by his first son and agreed to hand control of the Central Land of the Reed Plain to majestic Amaterasu. Afterwards he built the great Taisha Shrine of Izumo. The divine emissaries Takamimusubi and Kamimusubi returned to the calm of the celestial realm to report to Amaterasu that they had succeeded in bringing order and peace to the unruly lands below.

A 19th-century boxwood carving depicts a wrestler performing a *kawazu* throw. Such bouts originated as divine contests.

The Coming of Honinigi

Amaterasu had gained control of the Central Land of the Reed Plain and wanted to send a representative of her divine family to rule there. Her choice fell upon her grandchild Honinigi, who would be the ancestor of Jimmu, Japan's legendary first emperor.

Amaterasu called Honinigi into her presence and explained her divine purpose. In an auspicious ceremony she gave him three sacred objects that would become the symbols of imperial power in Japan. The first was the sword, Murakumo, that Susano had cut from a tail of the dragon Yamata no Orochi (see page 55). The second was Amaterasu's *magatama* or string of beads, some of which had been consumed during the sun goddess's child-producing contest with Susano (see pages 39–40). The third was the mirror that the 800 myriad heavenly deities had used to tempt Amaterasu out of the heavenly cave with her own reflection (see page 44). Copies of these objects were traditionally presented to the new emperor when he came to power.

With many divine companions, Honinigi began the voyage to Earth, but they had scarcely broken through the clouds of Heaven when they encountered a fearsome deity blocking their path. He stood at the crossroads of the heavenly realm where eight roads met, and was of wondrous size, his back as wide as a great plain dissected by many rivers, his nose seven hands in length. From his mouth and his anus light poured forth and his eyes dazzled like a sacred mirror held up to reflect the morning sun.

Honinigi and his attendants were overcome with fear and they turned tail and fled – all save the dawn goddess Ama-no-Uzume whose lewd dance had caused uproar in Heaven at the time of Amaterasu's withdrawal into the celestial cave. She had boundless confidence in the power of her appearance to seduce and subdue any opponent. In some accounts Honinigi asked her to approach the giant because no other god was willing – and in any case he knew her provocative ways would disarm him. (Ama-no-Uzume is sometimes identified as Honinigi's brother.)

Forward went Ama-no-Uzume, twisting her body provocatively, intending to bring the fierce-looking stranger under her spell. As before she danced a striptease, pulling off her blouse to bare her breasts, then slowly sliding out of her lower garments. Her light laugh rang out like a challenge, demanding a response from the giant. Ama-no-Uzume's dance fired the deity with desire and his eyes sparkled more brightly than ever. But he kept a breathless silence. Then she demanded to know who he was, blocking the gods' progress across the High Plain of Heaven in this way.

At last he spoke, in humble tones revealing himself to be Sarutahiko ("Monkey"), god of the field-paths – and probably also a solar deity. He had heard that Honinigi was preparing to descend to the Central Land of the Reed Plain and had come forward to offer his services to Amaterasu's divine grandson as a guide. He was familiar with the islands that lay below in the sparkling sea and

An 18th-century ivory netsuke of a dragon with a jewel in its front claw and a sword in its tail is a reminder of Susano's find and the imperial symbols.

The Fiery Birth

The curse of Ihanagahime (see page 65) could not disturb Honinigi and Konohana on their wedding day. They were rapturously happy and joyfully consummated their marriage beneath a gentle moon.

Within hours the princess appeared to be pregnant, throwing Honinigi into a frenzy of doubt and jealousy – for he reasoned that the child could not be his and that she must have had a lover before him. His restless mind could not leave the subject alone and at length he confronted her.

Honinigi's accusations were groundless and only brought shame upon husband and wife. Konohana felt this keenly and was furious that he had doubted her fidelity; she stalked away in silence, plotting a way of proving her innocence.

Near the beach where they had first met and confessed their love for one another, she had a straw hut built. She declared loudly that she would prove her offspring to be those of Honinigi. When her time came to give birth she would go into the hut alone and set fire to it. If the babies emerged unscathed it would demonstrate beyond any doubt that they were under the divine protection of Honinigi's bright grandmother, Amaterasu the sun goddess.

Konohana kept her promise. When her labour was advanced she had herself shut inside the cabin. Then, with a dramatic flourish, she lit the straw walls of the tiny house. The flames roared and onlookers gave her up for dead.

But inside Konohana delivered three healthy children. The first, Honoakari, emerged when the fire was first lit. The second, Honosusori ("Fireshine"), was born when the flames were burning most fiercely. The third, Hono-ori-hikohoho, or Hikohoho ("Fireshade"), came forth as Konohana recoiled from the heat of the flames.

Neither the babies nor their mother were harmed by the blaze. She cut their umbilical cords with a knife of bamboo and nursed them. His wife's honesty proven, Honinigi rejoiced at the opportunity to make up for having stained her reputation and lovingly waited on her as she recovered. The sturdy children thrived: curiously, no further mention is made of Honoakari, but his two siblings would become heroes of the next cycle of the myth.

would be able to lead Honinigi and his companions to the choicest streams, coves and headlands. He begged to be given the honour of serving respectfully in this way.

Ama-no-Uzume saw that she had made another conquest. She was in any case impressed with the god's body and lingered a while to enjoy his company, coming so close that her sweet breath passed alluringly across his cheek and neck. Then, bidding him a tender farewell, she returned to Honinigi and the assembled gods to reveal Sarutahiko's offer.

The Gods Travel to Earth

Ama-no-Uzume's news brought joy to the celestial company, and Honinigi happily ordered his companions once more to proceed on their way. Accepting Sarutahiko's proferred services, they continued with him as their guide. They traversed the bright celestial plain and descended onto the Floating Bridge of Heaven – where they paused to enjoy the view of wide sky, scudding clouds and sunlight sparkling on the waves around the islands of Japan. At last they moved on and came to Earth.

The place in which they found themselves was Mount Takachiho in Kyushu island's Hyuga region. From there they set out to explore Japan. On their path lay great mountains and forests, headlands, beaches, waterfalls, clear and rapid streams, hot springs and groves where the blossoms seemed to weigh down the branches. Honinigi was delighted with his inheritance.

When they came to Cape Kasasa, he determined to have a splendid palace built by a grove of trees. Honinigi decided to reward Sarutahiko for his service by offering him the hand of Ama-no-Uzume in marriage. Sarutahiko's delight knew no bounds, and the seductress herself was pleased with the proposal. Without delay they celebrated their wedding in Honinigi's new palace.

Honinigi adored his colourful groves and later fell in love with Princess Konohana who could make the blossom appear. *Cherry Blossoms at Mount Yoshino* by Katsushika Hokusai, 1760–1849.

In some later traditions Sarutahiko was one of the phallic gods of the roads (see page 47), while in others he was considered to be guardian of the Floating Bridge of Heaven. His wife, Ama-no-Uzume (a prototypical *miko* or shrine devotee), was associated with health and happiness and was sometimes called Daughter of Heaven, or Dawn. During the Heian period, an *uji* or clan of court dancers called the *sarume* claimed descent from the couple's fruitful marriage.

Honinigi Falls In Love

Honinigi liked to walk abroad in the calm of early morning. One day as he wandered on the seashore he encountered a young woman whose beauty made him stop short. He fell in beside her and asked her name. She said she was Princess Konohana, who made the flowers of the trees blossom. Dizzied by her soft voice and delicate beauty, he at once asked her to marry him, but the princess said he must first ask her father, Ohoyama, god of the mountain.

Honinigi presented himself respectfully to Ohoyama. The father was honoured by an approach from the grandson of Amaterasu, but he felt it was more fitting for his elder daughter, Ihanagahime, to wed. Accordingly he invited Honinigi to a great feast and sent his daughters in to speak to the prince. He declared that if the prince were to choose Ihanagahime it would give her father great pleasure.

But the elder daughter was as ugly as Konohana was beautiful and Honinigi would not consider marrying her. When the rejected young woman saw his response, she turned bitterly away to spit, while the mountain god, understanding that there was no alternative, gave way to Honinigi's desire. That very night Honinigi and blossom-beautiful Konohana were wed in her father's palace.

Poor Ihanagahime was so shamed that at the wedding she declared that Honinigi had made a terrible error. If he had chosen her, she said, their children would have lived for ever like the unchanging rocks of the mountain. But since he had chosen her younger sister, whose beauty would one day decay like the blossoms on the tree, their offspring would enjoy only a short life. According to this tradition death came into the world on Honinigi's wedding day – although another story said that mortality was a curse laid on humankind by Izanami (see page 37).

Scholars have been troubled by the problem of why the myths describe Honinigi coming to Earth on Kyushu island rather than in the Yamato or Izumo regions. Some have suggested that the *Kojiki* and *Nihongi* authors wanted to suggest that the divinely ordained destiny of the tribes of Kyushu lay under imperial rule. Another possible explanation is that Kyushu lies closer to Korea, and hence to the invasion routes taken by ancient Altaic-speaking Central Asian horsemen (see pages 8–14). The conflict with the Izumo gods therefore mirrors that of the subsequent confrontation between the horse-riding invaders and the ancient Yayoi and Jomon peoples.

Fireshine and Fireshade

Honinigi's sons loved their homeland and the sea that bathed its edges. Honosusori had an affinity with the water and was a great fisherman; Hikohoho loved the mountains and was a passionate hunter. But one day each agreed to try his hand at the other's way of life and Honosusori exchanged his special fish-hook for his brother's bow and arrows.

Honosusori spent many hours in the mountains, but did not kill one beast. Hikohoho, although a patient tracker along the paths of the forests, found that he did not have the temperament for fishing – and for all the long afternoons he spent at it, caught not a single fish. They decided to revert to their normal activities, but when the time came to hand their tools back, Hikohoho could not find his brother's fish-hook. He tried making a new hook, but Honosusori would not accept it. He melted down his sword and made a great mound of snares to replace the original one, and presented

these in a winnowing dish – but still Honosusori demanded the return of his own special hook. Hikohoho humbled himself in profound apology, but it was all to no avail.

Hikohoho was downhearted and wandered along the seashore, where the waves' steady pounding was attuned to his mournful mood. As

The story of Hikohoho embodies the ancient relationship between the Japanese people and the sea. *A Fisherman Standing on a Rocky Promontory at Kajikazawa in Kai Province,* **from a series by Katsushika Hokusai, 1760–1849.**

he turned at the end of one circuit of the beach, he encountered a white-whiskered, frail old man by the name of Shiho-tsutsu ("Salt Sea Elder"). Asked what was the matter, Hikohoho told his sad tale. Then the old man of the sea smiled gently and urged Hikohoho to mourn no more – for he could, he said, set the matter right. Shiho-tsutsu took a black comb from the bag he wore slung over his shoulder and cast it down on the sand. It became a growth of bamboo, which the old man used to fashion a large basket. He made Hikohoho clamber into it, then set him floating on the sea, where a tide took him far away from the shore.

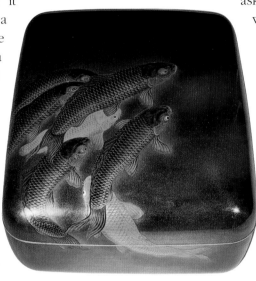

Alone on the waters Hikohoho might have despaired, but he trusted in the man's spell. In ancient days there was a watery passageway linking the seas around Japan with the kingdom of Watazumi, the sea god, and any mortals who chanced upon this channel would find themselves transported to a magic land deep below the surface. This adventure befell Hikohoho. He felt the basket to which he clung sinking like a rock, and then he was on the seabed, on a delightful sweeping beach like the very finest found on Earth. He clambered out of the basket and walked the wide sands until he came to the palace of the sea god. It was a great castle, with ornate gates, tall towers and forbidding battlements. Opposite grew a cassia tree next to a deep well. Here Hikohoho stood and waited.

Before long a maiden as beautiful as a glittering jewel emerged from the castle carrying a vessel encrusted with many gems. Hikohoho leaned against the tree trunk, allowing his eyes to feast upon her rare beauty. At first she appeared to be oblivious to his presence, but as she neared the

In Japan, fish species have acquired symbolic meanings, with the carp being revered for its bravery and strength. Rectangular document box decorated with seven carp, Meiji period 1868–1912.

well she did see him – and started violently before returning to the castle. There she told her father that a stranger of unusual beauty stood on watch opposite their retreat. As presiding deity of the sea, Watazumi had a great duty to provide hospitality, and so he laid out the best cushions and sent word to Hikohoho to enter.

The sea god treated Hikohoho kindly and asked what had led him to his watery realm. Hikohoho told the sad story of the loss of his brother's magnificent fish-hook. Happy to help, the sea god assembled all the fishes of the sea to ask if any had found the missing object. None had, but they did volunteer that one fish – the Red Woman, a tai or sea bream – had not obeyed his summons because she was suffering grievously from a sore mouth. When she was brought to the palace and her mouth was examined, they found the fish-hook caught inside it.

Hikohoho thanked the sea god graciously and happily looked forward to repairing his friendship with his brother. But he did not return at once to Japan, for his heart was troubled by love for the sea god's daughter, Toyotama ("Rich Jewel"). Fortunately, when he confessed his feelings it emerged that she reciprocated them and with her father's blessing they were married at once.

For several years, then, Hikohoho lived happily and luxuriously on the seabed with his bride. But dreams of Japan and her steep mountains troubled him more and more often. Despite his great love for his wife, he often woke filled with a longing to return home. Toyotama knew her husband well and guessed what was grieving him. She approached her father who agreed to let his son-in-law return to the Japanese islands.

Hikohoho riding on a mild-mannered *wani* or crocodile provided by the sea god to take him home, as depicted in a 19th-century print.

The sea god called Hikohoho to him and gave him the fish-hook, which he had been safe-guarding. He also made the prince a gift of two magic jewels, one with the power to increase the tide and the other with the power to abate it. Then Hikohoho went to take his leave of Toyotama. She told him that she was with child and would soon give birth. He should look out for her, she said, on a day of high winds and pounding seas when she would emerge from the waves on a beach near his palace. She would give birth on land in a hut he must build for the purpose.

Following his journey home on a tame croc-odile, the prince soon found himself treading the familiar stretch of beach near the palace. When he arrived back, the members of his family were amazed to see him after such a long absence. All gasped with delight and astonishment as he told the story of his adventures and happily presented the lost fish-hook to his older brother.

But Honosusori continued to harbour resent-ment against his younger brother and to treat him badly. Hikohoho therefore decided to make use of the magical jewels given to him by the sea god. One day as the two brothers walked on the beach, Hikohoho quietly crept onto the rocks at the back of the beach and cast the tide-raising jewel into the sea. The waves rose instantly, and Honosusori floundered in the deep water, calling desperately for help. When Hikohoho explained that he had magical stones that gave him power over the tide, Honosusori at once admitted being unkind to his brother and begged for his life. Hikohoho then cast the second jewel into the water and the tide left as swiftly as it had risen, leaving Honosusori

panting desperately on the wet sand, from where he cast a humbled look up at his brother. Some accounts relate that Hikohoho retrieved the jewels and was able to use them on many later occasions.

The stormy night that Toyotama had warned Hikohoho to expect came soon afterwards. Earlier he had built a hut close to the beach for his bride to take refuge in, and now he waited for her there. He shivered with fear, for lightning split the sky and thunder shook the night like an earthquake; the waves pounded the beach as if driven to fury by some quarrel raging in the natural world. Buffeted by the wind, Hikohoho stood forlornly on the beach for long hours. Midnight came and went and the prince was wet and chilled to the core. Then at last he saw Toyotama and her sister Tamayori emerge from the surf. They were calm amid so much turmoil and they approached slowly across the beach to embrace him.

Hikohoho took them to the birthing hut. Toyotama, saying she had arrived only just in time,

went in at once, warning her husband not to watch as she gave birth. But human curiosity tormented Hikohoho as he heard his wife's cries and he crept up to peer in through the loosely nailed planks. She was arched in labour, and he could scarcely recognize her, for she had taken the form of a green-scaled, long-tailed dragon.

Toyotama's head twisted in agony and her eyes locked with those of her husband. She said nothing, but he knew she felt very keenly the shame of his seeing her in her dragon form. The birth was successful and a bawling baby boy was safely delivered. But Toyotama reproached Hikohoho for having broken his promise not to look during her labour. Sadly she told him that it had been her desire to join the realms of sea and land for ever, so that sea creatures and people could move easily from one to the other. Now, however, she would merely return to the sea, leaving the child behind for him to love. Sea and land would forever be kept apart as distinct kingdoms.

Hikohoho bitterly repented his act of betrayal and begged his deeply loved wife not to go. But she would not be persuaded. She took the child, wrapped him in rushes and laid him tenderly on the beach. Then she walked into the water and closed the passage that had once linked Japan to the realm of the sea god. She was gone, leaving Hikohoho distraught on the beach and temporarily forgetful of the son who lay near his feet.

When he recovered he found that his wife's sister, Tamayori, had remained on Earth to help him raise the child. In time she became the boy's wife, and their marriage bore fruit in the form of many children, among them Jimmu of glorious reputation, founder of Japan's imperial family.

It was on a windswept beach that Toyotama gave birth to a boy who would become the father of Jimmu, founder of Japan's royal dynasty. This six-fold screen by Mori Ippo, _c._1847, contains the traditionally beautiful elements of white sand, pine trees and a gentle sea fading into the distance.

69

Jimmu, the First Emperor

Jimmu spent his youth on the western island of Kyushu where his grandfather Hikohoho had made his home. Later, as an adult, he called his brothers and children together and announced that he would continue the heavenly task begun by Amaterasu and extend the glories of imperial rule to the region of Yamato, on the island of Honshu.

In the *Kojiki* Jimmu is presented as a historical figure. In reality, though, he was legendary, and scholars cannot agree on the facts behind the myth. The traditional date given for Jimmu's accession is 660BC. Actually, the clan from which the imperial dynasty emerged rose to prominence in the fourth to fifth centuries AD; they are referred to as Yamato from the Honshu region of that name.

Some historians argue that the story of a migration from Kyushu reflects an actual movement by the ancestors of those who established rule in the Yamato region; others believe the dynasty rose to power there without any migration. More controversial is the theory that the invasion commemorated in the Jimmu legend was a historical one by Altaic-speakers from Central Asia.

According to the *Nihongi*, the emperor was forty-five when he began his journey of conquest and settlement. From Kyushu he proceeded resolutely, with great military might, by land and sea. On the waves Jimmu, at the head of a large fleet, met a deity astride a tortoise's back, who agreed to be his guide along the sea routes. In places Jimmu was welcomed and feasted by local rulers who pledged themselves to his service. Many harbours, rivers and settlements in Japan took their names from events that occurred on Jimmu's march. He met and subdued many deities who subsequently became the ancestors of important Japanese clans.

At the Hill of Kusaka Jimmu's troops encountered a fierce force, well led by Nagasunekiho, a local prince. It was a brutal battle, the armies were evenly matched, and Jimmu's elder brother Itsuse was wounded. Jimmu resolved to retreat, for the sun was low in the sky and his army was fighting into the sunlight, which was not fitting for a descendant of the sun goddess. He planned to attack at a later time in another place with the sunlight at their backs. It would symbolize for his men the great power of the goddess's dynasty.

The army accordingly withdrew and moved on. All this time, Itsuse was suffering keenly from his deep arrow wound. He did not pity himself, however, but donned heavy armour so that all could witness his bravery and recognize his steadfast spirit. But his strength continued to dwindle and finally, when the army came to Mount Kama, he died and was buried with great honour. Some scholars believe that in ancient tradition Itsuse may

Servant of Jimmu during his long trek, the tortoise is a symbol of longevity and a guardian of the northern signs of the Japanese zodiac. Late 18th-century bronze sculpture by Murata Seimin.

The Divine Lineage of the Emperor

By tradition Jimmu and his imperial descendants can trace their ancestry right back to the first days of creation, for Jimmu's ancestor was great Izanagi himself. Jimmu was linked to him through the descendants of Amaterasu, Izanagi's daughter, completing the confirmation of his legitimacy to rule.

Amaterasu's grandson Honinigi was sent to Earth bearing the three emblems of imperial power (see page 62). He fathered the prince Hikohoho, who travelled to the seabed and wed Toyotama, the beautiful dragon daughter of the sea god. Their son – born on the beach and abandoned at birth by his mother – later wed his nurse, Tamayori, who was Toyotama's sister and therefore another daughter of Watazumi. They produced many children, one of whom was Jimmu.

Wedded Rocks, located at Futamigaura in Ise Bay, gave shelter to Japan's first couple, Izanagi and Izanami. The sacred straw ropes symbolize the sanctity of marriage.

have been Jimmu's predecessor as emperor. (In the *Kojiki* the ideogram used to describe the moment of his death is the one reserved for the death of an emperor. Also, the fact that several generations intervened between Honiningi and Jimmu reflects a period of consolidation by the invaders in Kyushu before they went eastwards.)

Futsu no Mitama, the Wonder Sword

The army observed the proper period of mourning, then travelled resolutely on. After surviving a storm at sea, they came to the region of Kumano. There, as the men set up camp, they saw a great bear prowling close by; its roar made them shiver. That night terrible weakness afflicted the soldiers and their emperor, as if their food or the air they breathed had been poisoned. In truth the region's unruly gods had created a vapour that drained the men's strength.

But help was at hand from the army's celestial patron, Amaterasu. A man named Takakuraji had troubled dreams that night. He saw Amaterasu and a thunder deity, Take-mikazuchi, in conference on the heavenly plain. The goddess noted that her descendant was struggling in his divinely ordained task and urged her fellow deity to descend to Earth and pacify the emperor's enemies. Take-mikazuchi replied that he did not need to go down there himself for he could send his sword Futsu no Mitama; it would bring unstoppable force to the imperial army. Then he instructed the dreamer to look in his storehouse on waking the following morning, for he would find the sacred sword there.

Takakuraji did as he was told and sure enough found a great sword. Just as with the dual divine visitation to Okuninushi at Inasa (see page 60), the sword was somehow balanced on its hilt with the blade – sparkling with heavenly light – pointing upwards. He took it and brought it to Jimmu, who at that moment awoke from his slumbers. With the wonder sword the local deities were vanquished. Swiftly the army returned to strength and massed once more to march.

The Divine Sun Crow and the Dynasty

Jimmu's force climbed high into the mountains, but the route was so treacherous that they had to call a halt. Then Amaterasu intervened, appearing in a dream and promising to send Jimmu a divine guide in the shape of a red bird with three claws, named Yatagarasu or the "Sun Crow".

The crow descended and guided the imperial army across the peaks and slopes to the region of Uda, governed by two brothers named Ukeshi. Here Jimmu was greeted by the younger of them, who prostrated himself and revealed that his older brother was plotting to resist. He said that Ukeshi the Elder had raised an army, but on seeing the size of the imperial forces had been frightened and turned back. Now he had built a hall that concealed a murderous machine. His plan was to invite Jimmu to dine and then lead him into the room, where the device would end his life.

Jimmu sent a loyal soldier, Michi-no-omi, to reconnoitre. He encountered Ukeshi the Elder and denounced him for his treachery; then, enraged, Michi-no-omi drew his weapon and charged, driving the dishonourable Ukeshi into the hall he had prepared. Ukeshi blundered into the deadly machine and was killed. Michi-no-omi dragged out the body and hacked off its head, releasing a river of blood that lapped up to his ankles before draining away. Ever after the place was known as Uda no Chi-hara ("The Bloody Plain of Uda").

Ukeshi the Younger then laid on a feast of beef and sake for the troops, and Jimmu entertained his men by singing a traditional humorous song describing how each man gives his youngest wife the finest cuts of meat and expects the old wife to make do with a meagre serving.

Jimmu proceeded on his way, violently overcoming opposition and imposing the rule of law wherever he went. Finally, when he had routed all the enemies of order, he built a wonderful palace at Kasipara in Yamato. There he married a local beauty, Apirahime, but he still sought another maiden to be his principal wife.

One day he heard tell of a young woman named Isuke-yori-hime who had divine blood in her veins. The story was that her mother's beauty had drawn the attention of the god Omononushi. He could not forget her and followed one day when she went to relieve herself. Transforming himself into a red arrow, he fell into the water and was washed up beside her. She carried the arrow home, and that night she discovered that it had become a young man. She took him as her husband and their child was Isuke-yori-hime.

Another day, Jimmu met Isuke-yori-hime near the palace and was deeply impressed with her modesty and beauty. They began a courtship and in time she became his honoured wife, bearing him three fine sons. Many years later, after Jimmu's death, Isuke-yori-hime had to save their sons from the evil attentions of their half-brother, Tagishi-mimi, a son by Apirahime, who wanted to remove the boys to Yomi so that he could take power on Earth.

Unable to speak out openly, Isuke-yori-hime warned the children to be on their guard by singing songs about brooding nature and the massing of dark clouds on the mountain. One son, Take-nunakawa, then killed Tagishi-mimi and thereby saved the legitimate imperial line. As Emperor Suisei he succeeded Jimmu and consolidated the dynasty, which, according to tradition, has continued unbroken down to the present day.

Jimmu, with his divine crow guiding the way, delivers his people to their new homeland. Crows were revered in ancient Japan as messengers of the sun goddess. 19th-century Japanese print.

神武天皇

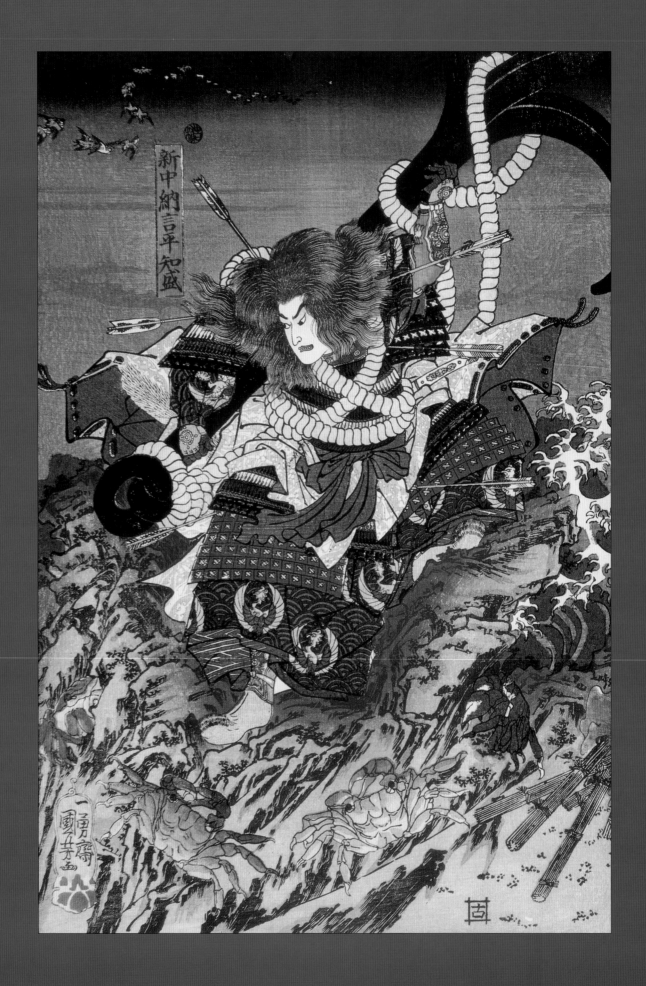

A NATION OF HEROES

Twelve hundred years and more after the *tennu* or emperor called forth a "divine wind" of war to blow away the Mongol invader, young fliers were finding inspiration in the word *kamikaze* for a tragic heroism of their own. Every one of the suicide pilots whose unavailing courage so unsettled their Allied enemy drew inspiration from the valour and self-sacrifice of a long line of mythic heroes. "The Japanese way of life is indeed beautiful", wrote one *kamikaze* pilot in his last letter home to his father: he was particularly proud, he said, of that history and mythology which reflected his countrymen's "belief in the past". There is nothing obscure or archaic about the tales of the Japanese heroes; modernity has not marginal-ized them: they remain central to their country's sense of itself. An identity formed through long centuries of isolation has now endured through decades of busy international com-merce. Japan is still a land of heroes where the names of the great warriors of the past live on.

In part, of course, their longevity can be attributed to the relatively recent passing of feudalism. Well into what the West would consider to be modern times, warlords held sway in Japan. A ruling caste of warriors naturally turned to tales of mythic heroism as marks of its own legitimacy. The samurai who exacted taxes and upheld the law locally, it was implied, was a direct descendant of those who had famously killed dragons and died for Japan. Religion said nothing to contradict this view. Shinto's insistence on the divin-ity of the emperor and, by extension, the sanctity of his samurai was only underscored by the influence of Confucianism, with its emphasis on social order and unquestioning respect for the sovereign power. Although out-wardly, of course, a creed of peaceful contemplation, Zen Buddhism also meshed easily enough with the Japanese warrior ethos. Waging war was, after all, only ever a very small part in the samurai's duties: the true samurai was gentle to those who were weaker than he, a fighter only for truth and for jus-tice. Zen's will towards mental discipline, moreover, could foster tireless training in the military skills, while its notion of transcendence of the self can be discerned in the tradition of heroic self-sacrifice, even unto suicide. History, religion and mythology have thus conspired together in Japan to guarantee the continuation of the cult of the hero.

Above: **A guardian at the Toshogu Shrine in Nikko, Honshu. It was built as the mausoleum of Ieyasu, founder of the Tokugawa shogunate. Heian era, 17th century.**

Opposite: **The gallant death of Tomomori at the Battle of Dannoura in 1185, the final battle between the Taira and Minamoto clans. Tomomori followed the child-emperor Antoku to his death rather than live to see his cause defeated. Colour woodblock print by Kuniyoshi, *c.*1844.**

Named in a Brigand's Dying Breath

Son of an emperor, Yamato-takeru was one of the greatest Japanese mythic heroes – and the most ambiguous. By turns he was a brave warrior and a squalid murderer, a chivalrous noble and a cunning cheat.

Among all the Emperor Keiko's eighty children, the two youngest – twin boys – stood apart in their nobility and their beauty. Identical in all respects, having shared even the same placenta, only a difference in character distinguished them. For the courage of the younger, though equal to his twin's, was rough and ruthless, and at times impetuous. So it was that one day, the elder twin having missed dinner several times in succession, their father asked the younger where his brother could be. He bade the boy tell his brother of his displeasure, and his insistence that he thenceforth be present at every dinner without fail. Mealtimes were important opportunities for the emperor to hold court before his family and vassals: in treating them casually, the young prince was delivering a significant slight.

Five days later, however, the truant had yet to appear: his father's fury could now scarcely be contained. Calling the younger twin before him, the emperor asked him whether he had spoken to his brother as instructed. He had indeed, replied the boy, and in no uncertain terms. Feeling a dark foreboding at these words, his father asked him what exactly they meant. He had waylaid his errant brother, the boy explained insouciantly, in the palace privy when he had come in to relieve himself first thing in the morning. Catching him unawares and helpless, he had killed him, torn up his body and done

away with it. The ungrateful miscreant would never treat his father with disrespect again.

Taken aback at his son's brutal loyalty, the emperor determined to find it some more appropriate outlet. There and then he resolved to send him down to Kyushu to put down the brigand bands which were disrupting the peace of that southern island. Before his departure, the prince offered sacrifice at the shrines of Ise, begging

Tales of Yamato, **a collection of 10th-century stories, from the series "Ten Designs of Old Tales". Woodblock engraving by Yashima Gakutei, *c.*1820.**

Amaterasu to smile on his undertaking. His aunt, high-priestess at one of the temples there, was delighted to hear of his mission. She gave him a richly woven robe of the finest silk and told him to keep it close by him wherever he went to ensure good fortune.

And so the youth set off to do battle, his fine wife Ototachibana beside him, a group of armed supporters in the rear. Down to Kyushu they went, only to find that their task appeared overwhelming: so strong was their enemy, so unaccommodating the island's rugged terrain. A pitched battle was out of the question, the prince saw: outnumbered – and, like as not, on such unfamiliar ground, outmanoeuvred – his little force would quickly be cut to pieces. His only conceivable option was to strike secretly at the heart of the rebel leadership. Yet this too was more easily said than done: the brigand chief Kumaso could be with any one of a score of scattered bands which roamed the island's impassable interior. By a stroke of luck, however, the hero learned that the enemy had been building a hall for feasting and were just about to open it with a massive banquet.

In Kyushu Yamato-takeru used the beguiling disguise of a pretty maiden to lower his enemy's guard. A portrait of a woman on a veranda tuning her *shamisen.* Toyokuni, 1769–1825.

Seeing his chance, the prince had his attendants bring him the robe his aunt had given him. Having bathed and anointed himself in fragrant oils, he then had his wife, Princess Ototachibana, help him put it on. Letting down his hair, he stuck it through with a pretty comb: a few jewels, a dab of make-up and, lo – the man was a maiden! Three well-armed ranks of brigands formed a ring round the banqueting hall – but a force which would have frightened an army held no fears for an attractive young woman. Such a fair creature needed no accreditation: she was welcomed unquestioningly to the celebration, Kumaso indeed insisting that she should wait upon him personally. Well schooled by his wife in the alluring ways of womanhood, the prince had practised the teetering steps of a delicate maiden. With fluttering eyelashes and demure downward glances he drove the brigand chief into a frenzy of desire.

Completely enthralled by this beguiling stranger, Kumaso could not rest without her presence: he kept draining his cup and recalling her just for the pleasure of seeing her standing by his side. Soon, inevitably, he was as intoxicated with alcohol as he had been before by the stranger's beauty. Only slowly did the rush of excitement give way to apprehension, therefore, when he saw the supposed maiden opening her gown. Craning forward eagerly to glimpse a woman's snowy breasts, he saw instead a naked weapon being drawn from his charmer's bosom. As the long knife glinted momentarily in the candlelight of the feast, Kumaso came groggily to the realization that he had been outwitted. Too late – the blade was buried deep in his body. Sensing that his life's end was upon him, Kumaso asked his killer who he was and where he had come from. When told that he was the emperor's son, the dying brigand asked if he could bestow upon him a new honorific name. Until that day, he told the prince, he had been held by all – including himself – to be, beyond comparison, the bravest and strongest man in all the country. Now, in his final moment, he knew that he had been wrong: from that time forth the prince should be named "Yamato-takeru", bravest man in all Japan.

The Grass-Cleaving Sword

Sent into the empire's eastern provinces to subdue the restless Ainu tribes or Yemeshi, Yamato-takeru was saved from certain death by the magic sword called Kusanagi, an imperial gift from the god Susano.

When a wave of unrest swept the remote eastern regions of his domain, who better to quell it, asked the emperor's advisers, than the conqueror of Kumaso? Prince Yamato-takeru was accordingly sent for and charged with the task of restoring order among the Ainu of the east, yet his father warned him not to expect an easy victory. The Kyushu brigands might have seemed like wild opponents, the emperor told his son, but they were tame beside the ungovernable Ainu.

Taking Retribution Against the Ainu

The Ainu's different manner of living antagonized the Japanese, for instead of erecting permanent dwellings they generally preferred a seasonally dictated nomadism, and their less hierarchical society – without recognized leaders with whom agreements could be reached – was regarded with contempt as anarchic. Their warlike abilities, however, and willingness to defend their way of life made them feared fighters on their own home ground. Such was their prowess that earlier emperors had preferred to turn a blind eye to their depredations. This passivity had merely encouraged them, though, and their perceived offences had only escalated. Now, normal life in the empire's eastern provinces was effectively in abeyance. In a series of increasingly violent raids, women had been abducted while their husbands laboured in the fields: the region's whole social and economic order was under threat. Yamato-takeru was to teach this enemy a lesson, the emperor concluded, but on no account was he to underestimate it.

Promising to do as his father commanded in every detail, the prince went again to the shrines of Ise. He told his aunt the priestess of his undertaking and this time she gave him that very same Murakumo sword which the god Susano had found so many centuries ago (see page 55), as well as a bag of loose flints which she told him he might at some point find useful. The sword being shapely and finely weighted, the young warrior did not need to be convinced of its worth. Why he should need the flints he could not for the life of him imagine, yet out of respect for the old priestess he took them with him.

A Japanese sword was held to be linked in some deeply spiritual way to its owner, and there are many historical associations with dragons – indeed, Susano found his sword in the tail of a fiery beast. This long, curved *tachi* has a dragon-headed hilt with elaborate silvered metal fittings engraved with a lacquered dragon and cloud design.

An Ordeal of Fire

Had Yamato only paid more heed to his father's advice, his campaign against the Ainu might have gone much more easily. Arriving in the east, however, he found a situation quite unrecognizable from the emperor's alarmist warnings. The last word in courtesy and urbanity, the Ainu made him welcome: no trouble, it seemed, was too great for their imperial guest.

After several days of friendly feasting, the prince was happy to accept his hosts' invitation to a deer-hunt in a remote region of the province. Here, the Ainu told him, there were deer of the greatest size and massed together in such abundance that their legs seemed a forest of tall trees, their breath combining to cloak the landscape like the mist of morning.

Anxious to try such bountiful hunting, the prince set off across the grassy plain all anticipation. He was far from help when he became aware of flames before him. Wheeling around in sudden alarm, he found himself encircled by high walls of fire, advancing steadily upon him across the burning grassland.

Realizing how easily he had been duped, the hero was on the point of despair, when he remembered the special sword and flints which he had been given by his aunt. Whipping out the flints, he quickly made a fire of his own, burning a protective ring round the place where he was standing, swishing about him with the sword at the longer grass. Now, hiss and crackle as they might in their frustration, the oncoming flames could come no nearer: Yamato-takeru stood there in safety as the blaze died in disappointment all around him.

So it was that, far from being baked alive, the hero emerged from the inferno unscathed, having scarcely so much as broken into a sweat. His

The Ainu's lifestyle set them apart from the Japanese, who derided their preference for fur over woven textiles and meat over cultivated crops. Handbook illustration depicting Ainu sledgers accompanied by their dogs in Kita Ezo Chibli, or northern Hokkaido, the last Ainu stronghold.

earlier credulity, however, had been well and truly incinerated: never again would he be so foolish as to trust his hosts. As for the Ainu themselves, they were so stunned to see the prince walk calmly forth from the holocaust's heart that they were thrown into consternation and confusion and fled the field, utterly demoralized.

But the hero's work was not yet done: he pursued them as they went – that his now-famous sword, renamed Kusanagi ("Mower of Grass"), could cleave much more than grass soon became all too bloodily clear. By the time the prince was finished, the whole province was strewn with the bodies of his enemy, the earth throughout drenched red. Yamato-takeru and his sword had slashed to shreds the foe's independent spirit.

Yamato-takeru's Twilight

Two tales of self-sacrifice complete the story of a flawed hero, redeemed by the sadness of his passing. First, his much neglected wife followed what she felt was the right path of dutiful marriage; then a chastened and mournful Yamato embarked on his final mission.

Yamato-takeru's courage in battle was never matched by chivalry at home: he treated his wife with indifference. In birth and in beauty Princess Ototachibana was one of the greatest ladies of her age, but Yamato-takeru regarded her with contempt. She bore his disdain with all humility and patience, never complaining at the daily slights, but merely striving harder to win his love.

Her husband's constant attendant through the years of campaigning, Ototachibana felt her youth ebbing away inexorably as the harsh sun of 100 route marches blasted the unsurpassed beauty from her face. A kind word or a tender gesture

would have more than made up for all that she had lost – and yet not even these were forthcoming. Ototachibana's bravery was equal to her sadness, however, and she always managed a smile.

Even when, on his way to put down another Ainu rising, her heedless husband met and fell in love with Princess Miyazu, Ototachibana succeeded in keeping her sufferings from the world. Miyazu had all the girlish grace and beauty which once had been Ototachibana's own, and Yamato-takeru's admiration for her broke Ototachibana's heart. Yet still she smiled stoically on as her husband promised Miyazu he would soon return to take her for his second wife. First, however, he had a hero's work to do – and for that, of course, he needed the long-suffering Ototachibana.

At Idzu's shore they saw the Strait of Kazusa stretching out before them. They needed to get to the other side if they were to reach the lands where the rebels were. His companions were nervous about the crossing, but Yamato-takeru derided their fears: this was no more than a little trickle, he told them – they could practically hop across. Shamed by his arrogant scorn the party put to sea without further delay, but scarcely had they left the shore than the spirit of the strait made his displeasure felt. A fearful storm arose out of nowhere to teach the boastful prince a lesson: mountainous waves washed over his craft; the wind shrieked dementedly, the lightning crackled and the thunder roared. To quell such a tempest a human sacrifice was required.

Yamato-takeru's lack of respect angered the spirit of the strait and it sent a powerful storm to endanger his frail craft. This woodblock print of a surging sea is from the series "Famous Places of the Sixty Provinces", by Hiroshige in 1853.

An Ignoble Deed?

Yamato-takeru's accomplishments, although undoubtedly great, frequently fell far short of modern ideas of courageous nobility.

His victory over one brigand chief, Izumo-takeru, was achieved by what now seems shabby subterfuge, the prince having contrived to get close to his quarry with protestations of undying friendship.

The infamous outlaw's confidence thus won, Yamato-takeru secretly fashioned a wooden sword, which he wore in his own scabbard in place of his real one of hardened steel.

One hot afternoon when the sun beat down without respite,

Izumo-takeru suggested that they go swimming together in a nearby river. It was the moment for which the cunning hero had been waiting. As Izumo plunged heedlessly in, Yamato-takeru – who had lingered on the bank – went to the brigand's scabbard and switched swords with him. Their dip over, the prince suggested a fencing contest – just for fun. Izumo stood there waving his wooden weapon uselessly, while his "friend" cut him ruthlessly to pieces.

That her husband had caused the storm did not deter Ototachibana for a moment; nor did his years of ill-treatment. No sacrifice could be too great, she told herself, to save the man she had loved so thanklessly: she would give up her own life willingly, rather than have a hair of his head harmed. The mission for the emperor also had to be considered: its outcome must not be jeopardized, whatever might befall. And so the brave princess offered herself to the storm aboard a ritually laden raft which was consigned to the roaring sea. The waves rose to receive her and drew her down swiftly into the deep: no sooner was she gone than the seas subsided and Yamato-takeru's ship was able to make its way to the Kazusa coast.

But it was a different prince who put ashore. Awed at his wife's self-sacrifice, he was struck by how little he had ever given up himself. The rest of his life would be passed in the deepest mourning for her – but, as the fates would have it, his time was not to be long. Sent out by the emperor to free the people of Omi from the attentions of a

monstrous serpent, the hero dealt with it easily enough. Having strangled the snake with his bare hands, Yamato-takeru thought his work done; but the serpent was no more than a minion of a more formidable demon. That fiendish master had by no means finished with the hero: filling the sky with darkness and rain, it sent a sickness stealing through the prince's body. His strength draining steadily away as he went, he headed homewards to report to the emperor one last time, but as he crossed the Plain of Nobo he knew that his end had come. Time flashed by, he said sadly, like a four-horse carriage past a crack in a wall. He was never, he sensed, to have sight of his father again. He died in that desolate spot, his life given up for his country and its people, an all-too-human hero rendered magnificent by his own courageous self-sacrifice. Grief-stricken at the loss of his favourite son, the emperor had a tumulus built for him on the plain where he had died, but soon afterwards his body took the form of a great white bird and flew back to Yamato, the land of his birth.

Yorimitsu, Scourge of Demons

Fortitude and cunning combined in many of the great heroes of Japanese tradition, but none possessed these qualities in greater abundance than the incomparable Yorimitsu, who was called upon by the emperor to deal with the evil monster Shutendoji.

Under the virtuous rule of Emperor Ichijo, Kyoto should have been a happy and prosperous place. In fact, life was made wretched by the activities of the demon king Shutendoji ("Drunken Boy"), who lived on Mount Oye in a fortress garrisoned by devils. Any impression of innocence created by his little boy's face was corrected by a giant's body clothed in a blood-red cloak. All too often he and his devilish followers ventured forth to ravage the whole region, spiriting away human plunder to their mountain stronghold. There, after torture, the captives would be torn apart and devoured.

The monster respected neither rank nor status, and the emperor decided that Shutendoji must be tackled once and for all. Only one man was deemed capable of such a challenge: Yorimitsu.

Stealth and Disguise

For the epic quest of tracking down and destroying Shutendoji, Yorimitsu chose five friends to accompany him. Such was the enemies' power, he told them, that they could not realistically be met in mortal combat: deviousness was going to be required. He was therefore asking them, he said, to dress in the robes of wayfaring priests, keeping their weapons well out of sight of their foe.

The six set forth after making pious observance at certain shrines, seeking divine protection for their perilous undertaking. Two prayed at Hachiman's temple and two at Kannon's, while the remaining pair went to the temple of Gongen. Thus spiritually equipped for the struggle ahead, they rode out intrepidly into the hills, arriving at length at the base of soaring Mount Oye. Dense forests and roaring torrents barred the way through its foothills, but just when the heroes were beginning to feel discouraged, three old men appeared: the very deities to whom they had paid homage before leaving home. They gave Yorimitsu a jar of enchanted sake, and told him to offer it to Shutendoji; he would find it packed more of a punch than he ever bargained for, they said. The gods then vanished, but the jar of sake was real enough. Emboldened, the men proceeded upon their way, plunging undaunted into the woods.

When they emerged above the treeline, they came upon a maiden in tears who had seen a friend eaten alive by Shutendoji and his companions. A princess in the world below, here she was a slave: different rules applied in Shutendoji's territory, she told them. When they then revealed their true purpose she rejoiced, but it was obvious she doubted their ability to succeed. She agreed to conduct them to the tyrant's lair, however, and set off ahead of them up the treacherous path.

The deity Kannon in robes and a headdress, carrying a drum and drumsticks. Bronze pendant, 19th century.

The Skull and the Spider-woman

The chronicler Kenko Hoshi's tale of the "Skull and the Spider-woman" shares many of the basic components of the Shutendoji myth, but it differs sufficiently in its details to amount to a separate story in itself: one of the most sinister and disturbing in all Japanese mythology.

By Kenko Hoshi's account, Yorimitsu was riding out with Tsuna, his most trusted companion, when they were both amazed to see a skull before them, floating along as if blown by the breeze. Following it across the plain for some considerable distance, they were still more startled to see it disappearing through the open door of a ruined mansion which neither had ever seen or heard of. Within was a wizened, white-haired crone, her eyelids falling back over her head like a hat while her breasts hung below her knees: the very picture of hideous decrepitude. She was 290 years old, she told them, housekeeper to a mansion full of demons – and as the men listened, they could indeed hear the ghostly footsteps of a great host of evil spirits.

Yorimitsu was making for his sword as if to defend himself, but suddenly he froze at the sight before him. Where an ugly hag had been was now the most beautiful maiden. Long seconds he stood there in dumb amazement before he realized that his temptress was busily enveloping him with sticky gossamer. He stabbed her with his sword, but she vanished clean away. With Tsuna's help he went searching through the ruined building until they found

a giant spider in a corner of the cellar. It lay sick and wounded, a broken-off swordpoint embedded in its body. Looking down at his own weapon, Yorimitsu saw that the tip was missing: this monster was the

maiden who had come so close to catching him in her web of charm. Dragging her out from her lair, the heroes killed her and, cutting her thorax open, they found there the remains of thousands of human victims.

In time they reached a palace of the blackest iron. The demonic sentries at the gate surveyed the group with baleful eyes. But when the girl told them she had brought back a lost party of priests, they smirked wickedly and waved them inside. Ushering them through a maze of passages, the maiden brought them to the banqueting hall. Yorimitsu did not know whether to laugh or to tremble when he saw the grotesque Shutendoji.

The king reacted to their coming rather as his guards had done, smiling sardonically as he bade the priests welcome to his humble home. Would they sit with him, he asked, and share the simple repast he offered? He clapped, and a host of servants sped to heap the board with sumptuous fare. Yorimitsu was shocked to find himself waited upon by the sons and daughters of Kyoto's noblest houses, but the hero knew he must keep his outrage to himself. Quietly, therefore, and with a politeness to match Shutendoji's own, he took the sake the gods had given him and offered it around. The company all took a cupful, and pronounced it very fine. So palatable did they find it indeed that they were soon pressing for more.

Soon the whole party was in boisterous mood, singing more raucously by the minute – and still the sake did not run dry. Before long they had all slumped into a stupor. Once they were satisfied that their enemies were asleep, Yorimitsu and his men donned their arms and armour – and at just that moment the three gods appeared again. They had bound Shutendoji's hands and feet, they said: the heroes should not fear the task ahead of them. While his men cut off the demon king's limbs, Yorimitsu himself should sever his head to complete his execution. That done, the deities said, it would be a matter of picking off Shutendoji's followers one by one. Having spoken in guidance, the gods vanished once more. The warriors were left to confront their enemies.

As instructed, Yorimitsu brought his blade crashing down on the demon's neck. As blood spurted forth from the wound, smoke and fire poured from Shutendoji's nostrils; his sword-hand singed, Yorimitsu found himself instinctively

recoiling. The heroes looked on, frozen with terror as, undefeated although severed from its body, the head hovered in the air, spitting blood and snorting fire. Recovering themselves, however, they created a flurry of steel no foe could have hoped to withstand. As the head fell lifeless onto the floor, the heroes slashed away and cut the demon's body to shreds. Shutendoji's waking minions were too groggy to defend themselves and were annihilated. The captives poured forth from the castle and fled down the hillside to home and freedom.

Yet even now the demons had another trick in store. Not long afterwards, back at the imperial court, Yorimitsu was taken ill. Each night a young

Yorimitsu's companions entertain themselves, unaware of their sick master's ordeal at the hands of the spider demon. Woodblock print by Utagawa Kuniyoshi, *c*.1838.

attendant brought him medication, and yet his condition worsened. At last the hero grew suspicious and asked his chief steward about the boy who was coming to his bedside. He found that nothing whatsoever was known about him: the "devoted" youth could well be a malicious impostor. When he appeared the next night, Yorimitsu did not drink the medicine he brought but hurled the cup at his head. The boy threw something small at Yorimitsu as he turned and fled. A sticky web engulfed the hero, and he flailed helplessly about in its gossamer folds. Yorimitsu's steward heard his cries, however, and managed to intercept and stab the attacker before he too was enveloped.

Finally escaping, he cut his master free, and then together they followed the blood-trail to a corner of the castle where the wounded creature skulked in hiding, severely weakened by the steward's sword-thrust. The demon spider was dispatched, and immediately the sickness passed from Yorimitsu. Only now, with the spider's death, was the empire finally released from the demons' attentions. But free at last it was, and the remainder of Ichijo's reign passed in peace and prosperity.

85

Ojin, Mortal Hero and Mighty God

So great was the glory of Emperor Ojin that he finally attained the immortality of a mighty deity: the proud figure of Hachiman, god of war. Hachiman is still honoured in Shinto to this day, when youths celebrating the attainment of manhood at the age of twenty invariably attend one of his many shrines.

Yet Hachiman, most formidable of the gods, came by his divinity only after a humbler, human existence, for he came into the world a mortal – albeit one descended from royalty. Born to Emperor Chuai and the warrior-empress Jingo, Ojin was marked out from the first for martial greatness.

Ojin's mother led a successful but lengthy military campaign against Korea in the fourth century AD, during the course of which it was said she carried a rock on her belly to prevent her pregnancy coming to full term. This miraculous gestation – three full years in the womb – allowed the fierce conquerer precisely the time she needed for the subjugation of her enemies. Just below the elbow of the newborn child, moreover, a strange patch of raised skin could be seen, in shape just like the little leather shield which protects the archer's forearm from the bowstring. Jingo delighted in a deformity at which another mother might easily have wept: for her it bespoke the military prowess she felt any son of hers ought to have. She was not to be disappointed: as the baby grew to manhood, all the world came to ring with the fame of his deeds.

The spirit of the legendary emperor Ojin lives on as the Shinto war god Hachiman. Associated with victory, he is worshipped by many non-military people in search of success.

Consolidating her own achievements, Ojin brought all the surrounding lands under Japanese sway.

Yet the emperor was also famed for his intelligence and wisdom, while he was as noble a practitioner of love as of war. His martial prowess and amatory ecstasy came together when he marched into the province of Afumi. Even before he was born, a prophecy had promised Ojin a land as beautiful as a lovely woman: at his first sight of the Kazu region, he thought he was going to swoon. With its lush green fields and neat little houses, the emperor had never before seen anything half as fair. As he approached the village of Kohara, however, he saw a maiden standing at a fork in the road: all the loveliness of the landscape seemed to come together in her beauteous form. She told him her name was Princess Miyanushiyakahaye, daughter of the local ruler. The emperor was enraptured and went to the house of the princess's father to beg for the honour of her hand.

His loyal vassal freely granting him what he asked for, the emperor burst into song – by what miracle of good fortune had he found himself in possession of such a paragon as this? How his heart overflowed with joy to have her at his side.

In payment for this boon of a bride as appealing as the lovely land, the prophecy had demanded something in return: the sacrifice of the ship used to transport the imperial ruler. Ojin's mother hesitated to comply with this request, however, feeling that she needed the craft to get about. It was to be Ojin himself who brought the prophecy to fulfilment when he noticed, late in his reign, that the ship was getting creaky. But he was reluctant simply to replace such a potent symbol of Japanese power. After great thought and prayer, therefore, he had the ship reverently broken up into firewood, which was then piled up and set alight beneath a vast vat of brine from the eastern sea. After many days and nights there remained in

the vat just a huge heap of salt which the emperor ordered to be shovelled into baskets – 500 in all. He then sent the portions out to every province of the empire as a token of their ruler's love. Overwhelmed by the gesture, each province built a ship as a mark of its gratitude: the sacrifice of a single ship was thus compensated 500-fold.

Ojin died around AD394, yet as far as the chronicles of Japanese mythology are concerned his life did not end there. Instead, while his body was laid to rest, his soul ascended to the heavens, assumed into the pantheon of deities as Hachiman, god of war. He was only the first of many heroes to attain such apotheosis: not only emperors but priests and even statesmen and scholars have traditionally been elevated to divine status since that time.

The Warrior Queen

One of Japanese mythology's greatest heroes was in fact a heroine – Ojin's mother Jingo, the warrior queen. When her lord Emperor Chuai died before his planned invasion of Korea could become a reality, his widow threw herself with enthusiasm into the completion of his work.

That the gods favoured her imperial mission was clear from their intervention in the course of her pregnancy: Chuai's son Ojin, the future emperor, lay three full years in her womb before being born, a delay which enabled his mother to devote her entire attention to military campaigning.

She was assisted further in her endeavour by her possession – like Hikohoho (see page 68) – of the Jewels of the Sea. By the use of these priceless gems, Empress Jingo's seaborne assault proved utterly irresistible: for the gem named Tide Ebbing was

used to strand the defending Korean fleet, while Tide Flowing was then used to drown the disembarked warriors. Resistance broken, soon all Korea was conquered and its kings pledged fealty to the Japanese emperors until that day when "the sun rose in the west, the rivers turned backwards in their courses and the pebbles from their beds ascended into the heavens to shine as stars".

Japan's first empress, Jingo, is said to have ruled in the 3rd century AD. She is pictured here with one of her ministers in a woodblock by Kunisada.

The Masterless Samurai

If mythic mortals could become gods, real heroes could win legendary status, a phenomenon most vividly illustrated by the celebrated story of the forty-seven *ronin* who avenged their insulted master and willingly paid the ultimate price for their disobedience.

The further it is followed back, the less clear-cut does Japanese history become, so inextricably are factual events intertwined with traditional myth. Yet even in more modern times, the boundaries between the two areas can be blurred. The story of the forty-seven *ronin* is a case in point. The main outline of the narrative is attested by historic sources, for these events happened as comparatively recently as 1702. Originally just an ugly incident at court, it has been transfigured by legend into an inspiring tale of human heroism.

It all began when the shogun chose two lesser lords to receive an important messenger from the imperial court and asked an official, Kira Kozukenosuke, to train them in the necessary protocol. The vain and avaricious courtier did as he had been ordered and his grateful students gave him the customary gifts in return, but he felt he had been poorly rewarded. Indignant, he started to blacken their characters about the shogun's court: they were vulgar, ill-educated and poor. One lord made a secret payment to Kira Kozukenosuke and the muttering about him stopped, but the campaign against the other, Asano, intensified. One day a gibe spoken to Asano's face provoked him beyond endurance and he nicked his persecutor with a knife. Although the wound was trivial, its symbolic force was graver. The attack had taken place within the sacred precincts of the shogun's court: only Asano's death by *seppuku* could atone for such a defilement. Whatever sympathy there might be for him, his guilt could not have been clearer; Kozukenosuke was the shogun's representative.

The forty-seven masterless samurai or *ronin* led by Kuranosuke attacking the mansion of the official who dishonoured their late *daimyo*, Asano. Print by Hiroshige, 19th century.

Asano knew his duty and without repining he used the same knife to ritually disembowel himself as the law demanded. His faithful retainers were now *ronin* – samurai left leaderless by their lord's death. What else could they do but disband and go their separate ways? They had no business questioning the judgements of the law, and in any case Kira Kozukenosuke, braced for revenge, had surrounded himself and his house with a large guard. So the forty-seven men who had served Asano so long split up and dispersed throughout the country. Some enlisted in the retinues of other masters, others became merchants and pedlars – even common labourers, all self-respect apparently evaporated since their lord's dishonour. As for Asano's closest companion, Kuranosuke, his whole life seemed to have fallen apart: once a disciplined warrior, he gave himself up to drink and debauchery. A coward and a schemer, Kira Kozukenosuke could not lightly shed his fears of an attack, yet the reports on Asano's men were unanimous in assessing they were not a company from which anything needed to be feared.

Unbeknown to the official's agents, however, Kuranosuke was leading his comrades in a long and cunning game. Although his own wife was so convinced by his performance that she took his children and left him in disgust, his abandoned life was all an act. As for the others, they had secretly remained in contact, gathering information and planning strategy, their lives all directed towards one single end: revenge. Unnoticed due to the strength of Kira Kozukenosuke's contempt, some of the warriors in menial occupations were even now at work in his own house; others, as pedlars, had been getting to know his staff.

As a result of such secret reconnaissance the men had all the inside information they needed when finally the time came for their attack. On 14 December 1703 the forty-seven *ronin* appeared abruptly from a driving snowstorm to assault Kira Kozukenosuke's sanctuary. Caught by surprise, his men were ill-equipped to resist: although many fought bravely, they were no match for Kuranosuke's little band of heroes.

In the moment of victory, however, they realized that their quarry had eluded them: their long months of self-sacrifice had apparently been in vain. Searching the house from top to bottom, they finally found Kira Kozukenosuke skulking dishonourably in a store. The brave forty-seven arraigned him with his crimes: now it was his turn to commit *seppuku*. But he was too craven for a warrior's death, and they ended up dispatching him themselves. Cutting off his head, they bore it in triumph to Asano's tomb. Their master's death was avenged and their humiliation forgotten. Sadly, however, honour demanded that they too kill themselves. This the heroes did and were buried with their lord in Gotokaji Temple, Tokyo.

Theatres of War

The forty-seven samurai recur in Japan's dramatic arts, for the stage has played a vital role in keeping the heroes of history firmly in the forefront of popular consciousness.

The stately, stylized *Noh* theatre – Japan's crowning cultural glory, some claim – developed in part out of the epic recitations of the strolling medieval story-tellers. They accompanied their performances with crashing chords on the *biwa*, a stringed instrument similar to a European lute: theirs was a declamatory style well suited to the warlike stories they drew from a repertoire rooted in the oral traditions of a much earlier age. That the *Noh* drama eventually passed into the custodianship of the samurai order did nothing to diminish its preoccupation with the warrior virtues of bravery and self-sacrifice. An aristocratic form aimed at an educated audience, *Noh* tends to focus on the elevated emotions and reflective meditations of its protagonists. The more spectacular *Kabuki* betrays its origins in popular puppet theatre in its taste for rumbustious, exciting action. It too draws much of its material from mythology, however, and in particular from the deeds of the heroes.

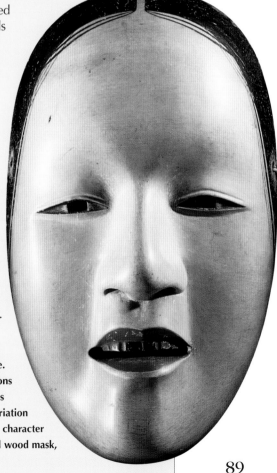

Noh masks are imbued with mystic significance. They are always variations on a type and the actors bring them to life. A variation on the "young woman" character is shown in this painted wood mask, 18th–19th century.

Momotaro the Peach Boy

A wholly fictional product of Japan's rich folktale tradition, Momotaro displays the same qualities of courage and nobility as the semi-historical heroes of the great myths, seeking to overturn the injustices suffered by innocents at the hands of rapacious demons.

Young Momotaro, carried by his foster mother who holds a peach bough. Ivory netsuke, 19th century.

An old woman and her husband lived happily together in a cottage in the mountains – happy, that is, in everything except that their marriage had never been blessed with a child. For years they had prayed to the gods to end their infertility, but as youth gave way gradually to age and the woman went past her childbearing time, they finally had to accept that they simply were not destined to be parents. One day, however, while the woman was washing clothes in the river, she looked up to see an enormous peach bobbing downstream towards her. Delighted at the thought of the fine dinner it promised for poor countryfolk such as themselves, the old woman reached out and pulled it into the bank, before bearing it off home in triumph. Her husband was as staggered as she had been to see the peach, and he too was excited at the thought of the meal it would make. Unable to contain his impatience, he took out a knife and was about to cut the peach open, when suddenly it split of its own accord and a tiny baby tumbled out. The child told the awestruck couple not to worry: he was a gift from the gods, he said, sent to comfort them in their childlessness, and to keep them in their old age. Overjoyed, they embraced their new son; Momotaro, or "Peach's Son", they called him.

Momotaro flourished in their loving care: he grew tall and strong, and with a well-developed sense of truth and justice. By the age of fifteen, he was already a man, with a hero's passion to go out into the world and fight for right and honour. One afternoon, accordingly, he came to ask his foster-father for his permission to go off on a quest. A horde of *oni* had for some time been roaming the countryside around, abducting the daughters of innocent folk and taking them back to their island lair, where many were killed and eaten. It was his intention, Momotaro told his astonished father, to search for these devils and put an an end to their reign of terror.

The old man listened with amazement to his son's request. He was certainly concerned to hear him outline such a hazardous plan, and yet at the same time he felt great confidence in the boy's abilities. Had he not been sent by the gods? And had he not shown superhuman powers of strength as well as wisdom well beyond his years? Why, then, should he deny him his permission for the scheme? If Momotaro could indeed rid the land of *oni*, the whole country would have cause to be thankful: thus he gave his blessing freely and wished the youth luck with his noble undertaking.

Both parents bid Momotaro a tearful farewell. His mother pressed upon him a number of rice cakes for his journey: he thanked her kindly before setting out. He had not gone far when he began to feel the first pangs of hunger and sat down by a field. No sooner had he taken a rice cake from his bag, however, than a great dog came up to him, growling in menace and baring its sharp teeth as it demanded food. It could speak in human tongue, it seemed, but what it had to say was anything but civil: it would have the rice cake, it insisted, or the

The Miniature Hero

One childless couple, tradition has it, were so desperate for a child that they begged the gods to bless them with a baby – even if it were no bigger than the end of an adult's little finger.

Listening in literal-minded spirit to their prayer, the gods responded by giving them Issun Boshi – a name which can roughly be translated as "Little One Inch". His parents were delighted, despite his minute size, and brought him up with every conceivable care until at the age of fifteen he announced his intention of going out into the world to do heroic deeds. His mother having given him a rice bowl and a pair of chopsticks, he used them as a boat and oars to make his way downstream; a needle and hollow straw they had given him he carried by his side as his sword and scabbard.

Arriving at Kyoto, then the capital, Issun Boshi entered the service of a noble family. One day he had to accompany the daughter of the house to the shrine of the goddess Kannon, where she wanted to pray.

When two evil *oni* attacked them, Issun Boshi hopped about furiously in an attempt to distract them. Seeing him, one devil reached down scornfully, picked him up and swallowed him whole. Drawing his sword and setting about him, the midget bodyguard caused the demon such unbearable pain from within that he coughed him up and spat him out before doubling up in agony.

Issun Boshi then leaped straight at the other demon's eye, where he once again put his sword to work.

Soon both *oni* were fleeing from the scene of the ambush. Leaping unhurt to the ground, Issun Boshi was receiving the thanks of his grateful mistress when they spotted a magic mallet the demons had left behind them in their flight. It was a lucky mallet indeed: if banged on the ground it granted a wish. Issun Boshi's lady did so, wishing that her retainer be a normal size. All of a sudden, there stood her champion at her side, a full-sized samurai. They married, to live happily – and in his case heroically – ever after.

get over their jealousy and become friends. Scarcely had they done so than a colourful pheasant stopped Momotaro. It too made the request to enlist in his service. Glorious in its plumage, it seemed to put the dog and monkey both in the shade. Their jealousy awakened, they tried their level best to kill the interloper, but Momotaro stepped in to separate them, and an uneasy peace descended upon his little band. With each kilometre that they went, however, the spats became fewer, until by the time they reached the coast, the animals were the best of friends. Now, though, they faced another problem: how were they going to reach the island fastness? They could see the *oni*'s stronghold looming across a strait of decidedly choppy looking sea.

Momotaro looked about him for some means to make the crossing. It was not long before he had found a boat, lying upon the strand as if awaiting the hero's use. His animal helpers were by no means happy to board, but then neither would they have dreamt of deserting their master. So with many misgivings they climbed into the vessel and put to sea. Short as it had seemed from the shore, the trip turned out to be long and dangerous: mighty waves picked up their little craft and tossed it about. They all clung on for dear life, and just when they were beginning to despair of ever making landfall, they sighted the island.

Momotaro sent the pheasant ahead to herald their arrival, and to deliver a stern message to the demon king. Landing on the highest tower of the *oni*'s castle, the pheasant addressed the diabolical multitude below. It demanded their ruler's surrender and that of all the devils at his command; in token of submission, it said, they were all required to break their horns. The demons greeted his message with derisive jeering. Shaking their horns and their shocks of flaming red hair, they threw iron bars up at the bird, but he dodged them nimbly, swooped down and started to attack them.

traveller's life. The dog was taken aback to find the wayfarer unperturbed by the threat. Disconcerted now, it demanded to know whom it was addressing. On discovering that it was Momotaro, it begged humbly for forgiveness. Had it known it was speaking to the famous peach boy it would have conducted itself altogether more respectfully. The ravening beast of moments earlier was now the picture of submission; it pleaded with him to let it serve him with its life and with every ounce of its strength and cunning. Momotaro accepted and, after sharing his food with his new vassal, the two went together in search of demons.

A little further along the way, however, they came upon a monkey: it too begged the hero to take it with him as a retainer. It was only too evident that the dog was not pleased with this plan, but Momotaro agreed just the same. As he continued his quest his two supporters swapped jibes and snapped at one another, only slowly did they

Back at the beach, meanwhile, his lord had landed. Striking inland, the party found female help just as Yoromitsu had done during his mission against Shutendoji (see page 82). Two maidens cleaning bloody clothing told the hero they were the daughters of nobles reduced to captive washerwomen to the demon king, yet they were thankful even for this ignominious occupation, given that it had kept them alive so far. It could not be long, even so, before they too were killed and eaten. Momotaro burned inwardly with indignation to hear such a story of cruelty and dishonour.

Momotaro told them he would free them and avenge their wrongs if they would only show him a way into the fortress. The ladies led the party up a narrow path which wound through dense woods and up a slope to the base of the battlements. There they uncovered a hidden door, just large enough for them to squeeze through one by one.

Emerging on the other side, the assailants raised a shout that momentarily silenced the demon mob, which the pheasant's swooping dives had driven almost to a frenzy of frustration. In a trice they had recovered themselves sufficiently, however, to mass and charge at their new attackers. As the dog bounded into their midst, however, laying about it with its powerful jaws, many fled in terror, little realizing that they were running straight on to the vengeful blade of Momotaro's whirling sword.

Some demons made for the apparent safety of the battlements – only to find themselves attacked there by the monkey, which swarmed all over the castle walls and roof, chattering delightedly as it hunted down its master's devil enemies. It was not long before all were dead and, left alone with no force remaining to command, the demon king had no alternative but to surrender. He pleaded for

his wretched life, but Momotaro was implacable in his fury. He had shown no mercy, the hero said, in his many years of depredation and murder: he could expect no pity now that his evil force had been defeated.

Momotaro proceeded to tour the stronghold. In every room he found wretches, many almost maddened by their fear and grief and by the terrible spectacles of carnage they had daily witnessed. As Momotaro brought them forth into the daylight, many were too stunned to rejoice. As they trooped home, though, they gradually recovered their spirits, and it was a happy throng indeed which eventually arrived back in their homeland. At their head strode Momotaro and his trusty monkey; behind him the dog and pheasant bore the demons' looted treasure. This was destined to be given to the elderly couple who had given Momotaro so much: all acclaimed this merited reward for those who had reared their country's saviour.

Representation of an *oni* or demon. These giants were of various colours, with horns and sometimes three eyes. Of Chinese origin, belief in *oni* came to Japan with Buddhism, and this rosary-wearing *oni* placed on a rock is probably a parody of Buddhist iconography. Kamakura period, 12th–14th century.

Friends in Arms: Yoshitsune and Benkei

Although a historic figure, born in 1159, the real-life Yoshitsune is overshadowed by the mythic hero he was eventually to become. Yet even this figure pales into comparative insignificance beside that of his legendary retainer, Benkei, the warrior monk.

During the twelfth century Japan went through a turbulent period in its history. A weak court proved unable to impose any effective, centralized authority, so the country's leading clan warlords vied to govern in the emperor's name. The Minamoto, from the eastern region around present-day Tokyo, were the main rivals of the Taira, whose base lay further west. Geographically nearer to the capital – then Kyoto – and politically closer to the imperial court, the Taira were able to outmanoeuvre the Minamoto, finally contriving their complete downfall in 1159.

A murderous spree followed this coup d'etat as the Taira disposed ruthlessly of any potential obstacles to power. Yoshitomo, chief of the Minamoto, was inevitably first to die; many other leading members of the clan would follow him – but not his sons. Too young at that time to be considered a threat, they were banished to far-flung parts of the empire. Yoritomo, the appointed heir, was thirteen at the time of his family's catastrophe. It was not long before he was plotting their resurgence. Yoshitomo's youngest and apparently least significant son, Yoshitsune, was not even the child of his father's marriage. His mother, Tokiwa, had been a minor lady-in-waiting at court: the victorious Taira chief, Kiyomori, made her his concubine. Tokiwa had to accept her lot, but if she was compliant in body she rebelled in her mind, and she brought up her son to treasure his father's memory and to seek revenge.

Yoshitsune was taught the art of swordsmanship by the king of the *tengu* whom he encountered in a forest. *Minamoto no Yoshitsune*, by Utagawa Kuniyoshi, 19th century.

The Tengu Art of Swordsmanship

In the hope of ensuring that they never attained the military prowess to challenge him, Kiyomori sent the boys at an early age to Buddhist monasteries. There, he reasoned, a training as monks would iron out any warlike instincts they might have inherited. Such a precaution was far too late for Yoritomo, but it might well have worked with young Yoshitsune, had he not left home with his mother's words of vengeance ringing in his ears. A quick student, the boy delighted his teachers; but they were unaware that he had a very different side. His frail appearance belied the man's heart which even now beat in his chest. For at night when he was supposed to be in bed, Yoshitsune stole out alone into the woods, where he schooled himself diligently in the warrior's arts.

One night as he practised his swordplay in a woodland glade, a thunderstorm rent the heavens above him, and through driving rain and wind a grim figure descended before him. A giant bird-man with a red beak-nose, feathered wings and clawlike feet stood there, glaring at him from furious eyes. Unafraid, Yoshitsune simply asked him who he was and what he wanted. His visitor was in fact the king of the *tengu* – a breed of mischievous mountain elves (see pages 110–111) – and far from being annoyed at the boy's assurance, he laughed heartily at his boldness. He had watched him a long while, he told Yoshitsune, and would like to help him. The *tengu* would train him in feats of swordsmanship no mortal warrior had ever dreamt of accomplishing: it was no idle boast, as the hero's foes would in time discover.

A Mighty Partnership

The years passed, and when he reached fifteen Yoshitsune decided the time had come to travel. By leaving he was forestalling his final vows as a monk – undertakings which would have bound his hands as a warrior and ended any ideas of ever exacting violent vengeance for his father. As he travelled in search of adventure, he heard stories of a fearful warrior-monk, the sort of man against whom a hero's mettle might be tested.

Benkei, as this wild monk was called, was a real priest, and genuinely pious in his aims: he was bent on raising funds for the restoration of a Buddhist temple. His approach to this sacred duty was unorthodox, however: posting himself by Kyoto's Gojo Bridge, he waylaid passing warriors and relieved them of their swords. So far he had met 999 warriors and acquired 999 swords: 1,000 would give him what he needed for his temple. Yoshitsune decided to confront this priest. His

robberies could not be tolerated, the young hero asserted: he would fight him and kill him, imposing a monkish decorum upon him the hard way.

So it was that one summer's evening, as he stood at his post by the bridge, Benkei looked down the road to see a youth walking leisurely towards him playing a flute. The effete-looking

The Peerless Archer

Yoshitsune came from a long line of heroic warriors. His uncle Tametomo too had known both victory and exile. Renowned from boyhood for his skills as an archer, he led the resistance to the rule of the Fujiwara clan.

But when the Minamoto catastrophe came amid so much slaughter, Tametomo was banished to an offshore island, the tendons of his arms having first been cut to end his prowess with the bow and arrow. He had not been in his place of banishment long, however, when he seized power and established himself as king, to the great consternation of the imperial court.

The navy being sent to quell this insurrection, Tametomo took his force of islanders and went and stood on a cliff-top. He loosed off a single arrow as the fleet approached. Both sides watched in awed astonishment as the shaft pierced the imperial flagship: water gushed in through the resulting hole and the vessel quickly sank. The rest of the fleet was thrown into fear and confusion – what was to stop such an archer repeating his trick as often as he wanted? – but Tametomo wanted no more death or bloodshed and ordered his forces to retreat. He would not send defenceless sailors to the bottom in their thousands; neither, on the other hand, would he let the fleet force a landing and wreak revenge on the innocent islanders. He was the cause of all this trouble: it was he who should take responsibility and bear the punishment. So, withdrawing into the interior of the island, he committed *seppuku*, a brave hero in the great Japanese tradition.

figure did not seem to Benkei to warrant a second look, until all of a sudden he spun round and kicked the axe from the giant's hand. Enraged, the monk slashed out, but his target was nowhere to be found: Yoshitsune danced nimbly between Benkei's sword thrusts. He was soon as dizzy as he was wild with anger, but his opponent's teasing attack merely intensified. Finally Benkei collapsed in confusion, looking up to find his vanquisher sitting on his chest: he had been defeated without a blow being landed. None of his own strokes had even come close, while the youth had not even

condescended to draw his sword. The discovery that he had been defeated by a son of Yoshitomo did much to alleviate his humiliation: awestruck, he begged that he might accompany the younger man as his retainer. Thus was born one of the great partnerships of Japanese mythology; together the two would perform numerous heroic deeds.

The two friends fought as sworn enemies of the Taira clan, yet Yoshitsune had an even more implacable foe in the person of Yoritomo, his elder half-brother and the legitimate heir to leadership of what remained of the Minamoto clan. This was

The Ghosts of the Taira

Even in death the Taira clan found it hard to accept that they had lost their leading position. Tales abound of how their ghosts haunt the battlesites where they were defeated by Yoshitsune and Benkei.

Strange lights in the night still, they say, flicker on the waters of the Strait of Shimonoseki where the Taira were finally smashed at the Battle of Dannoura. Certain scuttling crabs frequent the shores here: the spirits of the Taira dead, reluctant, even now, to leave the scene of battle.

A blind lute or *biwa* player, Hoichi, was renowned for his renditions of the Taira story. He lived at the family's memorial temple by the strait. One night, an armed samurai appeared before him and summoned him to come and perform to a party of dignitaries who wished to view the scene of the ancient battle. The warrior led him to a large chamber

where an appreciative audience heard his recitation: there were many samurai, and fine ladies accoutred in the antique mode. Time after time thereafter he was called to perform again, until one stormy night a monk missing Hoichi from his room and fearing for his safety, started to search the temple for the old minstrel. He finally found him sitting on a stone monument in the cemetery in the bitter cold, smiting his *biwa* and declaiming his tales to an audience of Taira tombs. When the monk tried to get him to come inside, Hoichi reacted furiously: how dared he interrupt him before such a distinguished company?

Minamoto Yoshitsune and the warrior monk Benkei fight on Gojo Bridge in Kyoto. All sources agree that Benkei was a giant figure, but some also talk of his exotic origins as the son of a samurai's daughter and a *tengu* father. After thirteen months in the womb, he sprang forth with a mane of long hair, a full set of teeth and fully developed limbs. The scene comes from a mid-16th century scroll, *The Tale of Musashibo Benkei*, after the painter Tosa Mitsuhiro and calligrapher Imagawa Ryoshun.

never disputed by Yoshitsune and he fought loyally for the clan cause with no other thought than revenge for his father's murder. Yoritomo, however, was too mean-spirited to be able to conceive of such self-sacrificing service. He envied his half-brother's accomplishments, and when Yoshitsune had led the Minamoto forces to their first triumph against the Taira in dashing style at Ichinotani, Yoritomo could scarcely bring himself to express appreciation of this long-awaited victory.

Their defeat left the Taira utterly demoralized – and utterly defeated too, or so they might have been had Yoritomo been able to govern his envy and suspicion. Instead, however, he forbade his half-brother from following through as he had desired. Rather than afford him an opportunity to win further glory, Yoritomo summoned him back to Kyoto while the Taira gratefully regrouped. Another year would go by before Yoshitsune was allowed to emerge and face a newly ascendant Taira army again. Once more he showed his great bravery and tactical brilliance, using a small force to astonishing effect when he crossed the Inland Sea in a typhoon to take a vast army by surprise and rout it completely. Once more, however, he was denied the chance to consolidate the victory, Yoritomo ordering him from the field before he gained too much glory.

Thus it was that Yoshitsune was left to defeat the Taira for a third time. This time, though, victory was total. In the naval battle at Dannoura, in the narrow strait between Honshu and Kyushu, Yoshitsune cunningly used the turning tide to reverse the course of the battle against the enemy, who had seemed set to triumph over a smaller and less-experienced Minamoto fleet. The sea was dyed with Taira blood that day; the banners of their sunken ships flecked the water's surface like fallen leaves on an autumn pond. Yet the success proved the final straw for the envious Yoritomo: Yoshitsune and Benkei had to flee for the hills, finally committing *seppuku* when they found themselves surrounded. So ended the lives of two great heroes who, having so long survived the myriad perils of war, could not in the end prevail against a mediocrity's inglorious scheming.

Lord of the Rice Bale

The tale of how the hero Hidesato acquired the name of Tawara Toda, by which he would become known to posterity, is one of the strangest and most stirring in all Japanese mythology, involving the two ever-fascinating themes of dragons and monster-slaying.

One day as Hidesato was making his way round the edge of Lake Biwa, he found his way blocked by a river that had the lake as its source. The river itself was spanned by a bridge; more of an obstacle, however, was the sleeping serpent, vast and ugly, whose coils sprawled across the path before him. But Hidesato was not a man to let some monstrous dragon concern him: climbing up its slumbering form, he jumped down the other side and simply continued on his way.

A voice behind him causing him to look back, he saw instead of a sleeping snake a strange humanlike figure, with wild red hair on which a dragon-shaped crown rested regally. This unlikely apparition explained he was the Dragon King of Lake Biwa, and he needed Hidesato's assistance in a heroic task. For many years he had assumed his dread dragon form at the approach of any human stranger, but until now every wayfarer who had seen him so had run away. Hidesato, however, had proven himself a man without fear: he begged him, therefore, to stay awhile and help him free his kingdom from the tyranny of a huge centipede dwelling deep within nearby Mount Mikami. It came down daily to snatch the king's subjects, dragging them off to be killed and eaten. Even the royal palace was not safe: his children and grandchildren were being abducted by the monster. It could not be long before he himself was taken.

Accompanying the king to his home beneath the lake, Hidesato was staggered at the opulence of it all: its magnificent chambers seemed to shimmer in the soft underwater light. At the heart of the palace was a vast and luxurious hall, where the hero was invited to eat the choicest delicacies. As he supped the sweetest sake and picked at crystallized lotus flowers, a troupe of goldfish danced sensuously to the eerie music of a band of carp.

Entranced and slowly surrendering to the sake's embrace, Hidesato was suddenly jerked to alertness by what sounded like a mighty thunderclap. The king beckoned urgently, summoning Hidesato to a window that he abruptly threw open, ushering the hero on to a balcony from which Mount Mikami might be seen.

Might have been seen, that is, had its slopes not seethed from top to bottom in the thrashing coils of a giant centipede. Its 100 feet glowed like lanterns while the twin fireballs it had for eyes lit up the hideousness

A detail from a 17th-century scroll by an unknown artist showing Hidesato killing Mukade, the centipede of Mount Mikami. Part of his reward was an inexhaustible rice bale.

was broken only by jagged flashes of lightning. Fearful thunderbolts shook the earth and a terrible storm raged all night long, but the next morning's sun finally rose upon a scene of peace and beauty.

Hidesato was acclaimed as the saviour of the Dragon King's people. For many days and nights there were celebrations, but finally the hero announced that he must take his leave and resume his journey. The king would not hear of his departing before he had accepted certain gifts: a bale of rice, a roll of silk, two bells and a cooking pot. The hero donated the bells to a nearby temple to commemorate his achievement; the rest of the gifts he decided to keep for himself. And priceless presents they proved to be: the pot would cook without ever being placed near a fire, while the roll of silk disgorged the finest fabric without ever reaching an end. Best of all, however, was the magic bale of rice: year after year it yielded its rich grain without any sign of nearing exhaustion. That remarkable gift made Hidesato's fortune and gave him a new name: Tawara Toda, Lord of the Rice Bale.

of its giant head for all to see. Hidesato grabbed his bow, snatched an arrow from his quiver and sent it swishing through the water. To his surprise and consternation, however, it glanced harmlessly off the monster's head. He took aim again: once more the dart was beautifully placed – but once more it spun off without inflicting injury. The hero was growing anxious when he suddenly remembered an old story he had once been told about human saliva having magic powers: with this in mind, he licked his last arrow before loosing it at its target. This time the shaft sped straight to its mark and stuck fast; in dying agony the monster collapsed into a heap of lifeless coils. As the lights in its head and feet were extinguished, so too the sun's light disappeared from the sky: the blackness

Heroic Hidesato rescued the Dragon King of Lake Biwa from the travails of a giant centipede. Iron dragon produced by Myochin Kiyoharu, 18th–19th centuries, a member of a famous family of armourers.

99

THE WAY OF THE WARRIOR

Japan is a land of extremes: topographically varied and breathtakingly beautiful yet violently volcanic. For 600 years it was ruled by clan-based shogunates drawn from the samurai warrior class, men whose ethos derived from centuries of militarist values first articulated in the traditional mythic tales of warring clans, heroic leaders and feats of valour and endurance – particularly the idealized role-model provided by Yamato-takeru. They glorified war and fearlessness, emphasizing selfless sacrifice and total loyalty to one's lord or *daimyo*. But at the same time artistic culture was gradually encouraged to flourish and a governing class was set in place which enabled modern Japan to emerge.

The samurai class took centuries to emerge, but by the twelfth century the struggle for land ownership and clan dominance had resulted in rival, warring fiefdoms inspired by stories of their own historic actions. The First Shogunate (1185–1333) marked the onset of the samurai's domination of Japan. By the Third (Tokugawa) Shogunate *daimyo* power was being curbed by Ieyasu from the centre; at the same time a rigid four-class social structure was instituted, under the supervision of the emperor, with the upper class constituted by the samurai, presided over by the shogun. *Bushido*, a code developed in the mid-1600s, emphasized the duty of everyone to respect and honour those above them in the social pyramid. It built on Zen meditation's philosophical strands; advocating concentration, discipline and sudden inspiration, Zen had a natural appeal for men who made ready for battle by preparing the mind to transcend the fear of death. However, the total triumph of central control and consolidation of national unity sowed the seeds of the shogunate's destruction, for there were no battles left to fight. Slowly the system ossified before collapsing in the nineteenth century, although the tradition remained deep-rooted enough in the national psyche for the Mongol-defeating *kamikaze* or "divine wind" to be an inspiration into the twentieth century.

Above: Typical curving roofs and gables of a *tenshu* – a large tower of storeys of decreasing size built within a central compound – at 16th-century Matsumotojo Castle in northern Honshu. The *daimyo* protected their powerbases with the construction of vast castles or *shiro*, particularly during the Sengoku-jidai or Age of the Country at War (1490–1600). Early castles were built of wood, bamboo and earth, but prolonged war and the introduction of Western techniques of fortification led to increased use of stone and moats.

Left: Ornamental horns dominate the decoration of this 17th-century helmet made in the ancient style. It belonged to a member of the forces defeated by the Tokugawa in 1600 at the watershed Battle of Sekigahara, near Mount Ibuki.

Right: A 17th-century portrait scroll of Tokugawa Ieyasu, shogun from 1603 onwards. He moved the centre of power from Kyoto to Edo and consolidated the Tokugawa clan's hold on power. During the Tokugawa shogunate – a period lasting 265 years until the Meiji restoration in 1868 – the samurai dominated Japanese society.

Above: A sword fight between two retainers, by Utagawa Kuniyoshi, 1843–47. Swords were all-important to the samurai and good ones became objects of reverence and worship, imbued with mystical power. A sword was used for oath-taking as well as during rituals of birth and death.

Right: Statue of Saigo Takemori which stands in Ueno Park, Tokyo. Takemori was a highly respected samurai from Satsuma who helped to usher in the Meiji modernization of 1868, but he grew disenchanted with the speed and far-reaching scope of the changes. When sword-wearing was forbidden

in 1876 he led armed resistance to the new government. In February 1877 he and his 15,000 followers launched the Satsuma Rebellion but were driven back to Kagoshima and besieged by a much larger force. Wounded during the final battle in September, Saigo's life was ended by a faithful retainer.

Left: A samurai writing a poem on a cherry tree, woodblock by Ogata Gekko, 1895. During the long period of peace ushered in by the Tokugawa shogunate, the warrior class developed as much of an interest in the arts as in the waging of war. The crest of the imperial army was a cherry blossom, Japan's samurai having long identified themselves with the flower which quickly dies after a brief but glorious life.

Right: The centuries-long domination of Japan's warrior class encouraged the growth of a skilled class of armourers and craftsmen with unrivalled technical and decorative mastery of their art. This 19th-century *tachi* sword has been richly decorated with images of warriors from the Gempei Wars. Ivory hilt, *tsuba* and scabbard by Ungyokumon Sei.

SUPERNATURAL FORCES

The size of the crowd confirmed what all in any case knew: the dead man had been both loved and well respected. Here by the graveside as the priest intoned his blessing, the sons and daughters of the departed stood with children and grandchildren of their own. A little further off the late lord's household servants were assembled in solemn ranks, while beyond them his peasants prayed in a shuffling throng. Neighbouring landlords had come to pay their respects to one who had brought honour and prestige on their class; city dignitaries were here to bid farewell to an important local figure. There was even a court official in attendance to mark the passing of a devoted upholder of the empire. The turnout for the ritual obsequies was impressive, with only one significant person missing – the dead man himself, of whom neither coffin nor corpse could anywhere be seen.

But he, as all present knew, had in fact been the first one there. His body had been lying in an adjacent grave these three decades and more. Many of those who had known him in person had gone to join him in the earth, but their descendants did not question their connection with the dead man. So starkly did old Japan distinguish between the body and the soul that it ordained a separate burial for each, the spirit or *tama* continuing to frequent the body's old haunts for thirty-three years. Even when the spirit had finally been laid in the earth there would be no real finality about it: the person's particular ghost would become a more general ancestral spirit. In so clearly separating body and soul, paradoxically, this attitude ended up bringing them far closer together, peopling the world of mortal men and women also with living spirits. The boundary between "reality" and the "supernatural" scarcely existed in the Japanese mind, so readily did the souls of the dead transcend it. And where ghosts could freely rove, so too could other spirit-beings, endowing not only animals, but trees, flowers and even the weather, with benign or malevolent will. Nowhere is this more evident than in Japan's rich folktale tradition. Collected hundreds of years ago by medieval scribes and scholars, but treasured and retold right down into the modern age, these stories, by turns delightful and disturbing, reveal a natural world which positively seethes with supernatural life.

Above: **Some of the 1,000 *jizo* figures for which the Jomyo-in temple at Yanaka, Tokyo, is famous. Jizo, god of mercy and compassion, is the graveyard keeper who protects souls against evil spirits and guards them at night.**

Opposite: **Shoki the demon-queller holding a mischievous *oni* and a drawn sword. Ivory netsuke, 19th century.**

Duping the Devil

In the *oni*, dark demons of Japanese tradition, the diabolical and the ridiculous combine. With well-muscled flesh of an odd colouration and an overgrown face-splitting grin, the *oni* is both strong and menacing – but his physical power is matched by his stupidity.

A devil and his demon wife once lived in a cave in the mountains. Each day they would descend to the valley to snatch hapless humans for their food. Looking on from his shrine, the local deity Tametomo took pity on the people's suffering and, assuming human form, he went to tackle the demon couple in their lair.

Arriving at the cave, he introduced himself as a well-wisher. Why were they putting themselves to such trouble, he asked, to secure their supplies of human flesh? Such an inefficient system suited nobody. Instead, he proposed the following deal: If in the course of the next night they could build a staircase of 100 steps, from the valley bottom up to his shrine, he would personally guarantee that they no longer had to hunt for food. They would

A pair of powerful *oni* figures, their distinctive short horns emphasizing their demonic look. Made of hollow lacquer, 19th century.

have living men and women brought daily to their door. If they failed, of course, they would spare the villagers all future depredations.

The *oni* agreed, scarcely believing their luck at being offered such a service on such easy terms – and indeed Tametomo was taken aback at the effortlessness with which they set about the challenge he had set them. Tossing vast boulders from one side of the valley to the other as if they were weightless, they had all but finished the staircase in just a matter of hours. By midnight it was clear that the god had badly miscalculated.

Ninety-nine stone steps strode up the slope, coming within a few feet of the shrine, when suddenly a cockcrow announced the dawn. Wailing in disappointment, the demons threw their last boulder down in disgust. They had come so near their goal, and yet it was apparently not to be; they went off up the hillside disconsolate, and were neither seen nor heard of again. Back at his shrine, Tametomo sighed with relief. That pitch darkness still shrouded the scene – with no sign yet of imminent daybreak – had fortunately not struck the credulous demons as in any way strange. They had taken his imitation cockcrow for the real thing and allowed themselves to be easily bamboozled. Might all accursed spirits show such blessed stupidity!

Like the evil they so energetically embody, Japanese demons come in myriad different forms, from fearful giants the size of continents to puckish little practical jokers. One theme remains more or less constant: terrifying in appearance and behaviour though they may be, the *oni* remain in certain important respects reassuringly comic. The stereotypical portrait of the demon is a strange blend of the sinister and silly, his flat face slashed by an overgrown mouth that grins from ear to ear. Twin horns top a hideous head from which three eyes glower forth; three clawed fingers and toes disfigure his hands and feet. His naked flesh of pink, grey or even blue clashes with the tigerskin he wears round his waist. In his right hand, the typical demon wields an iron club crowned with lethal spikes; he draws a flaming cart into which he tosses the sinful souls of the damned. Yet, fearsome as he is, the demon's grotesqueness always tends to have an absurd aspect. His great strength is matched only by his gullibility.

The Devil's Bride

A beautiful bride was riding in a wagon one day towards the village where she was to meet her future husband. Suddenly a dark cloud came down and enveloped the cart with its lovely cargo, whisking them away into the sky as the girl's family and attendants looked on helplessly.

The bride's spirited mother set off alone in search of her beloved daughter. All afternoon she walked, until nightfall found her at a lonely shrine by a river. There the priestess not only provided her with a bed for the night but revealed to her the whereabouts of the missing girl. She was being held, the priestess said, in a castle across the stream, the unfortunate captive of a company of *oni*. There was a bridge across the river, but it was guarded by two giant dogs – she would be able to cross only when they were asleep.

Next morning the woman awoke to find herself alone in the middle of nowhere; shrine and priestess, it seemed, had been no more than an empty dream. Yet the river and bridge, she saw, were real enough; there was a pair of terrifying guard dogs, too – or at least they would have been so had they not been asleep. Encouraged by this hint of the vision's reality, the woman stole across the bridge and into the castle. There she found her daughter alone in a chamber, weaving.

A 19th-century painted scroll depicting a variety of painful torments being inflicted upon humans consigned to Hell.

Shoki, Devil-queller

Shoki, the devil-queller, is a popular figure in Japanese folklore: his image appears on flags raised at the May Day celebrations every year.

A key feast in Japan's religious calendar, May Day is the festival at which all evil spirits are banished for the year: wicked spells, curses, diseases and other devilry. Shoki, its patron spirit, is a relative newcomer to Japanese folk tradition, having originated in China during the eighth century. There, it is said, his career in the service of the Chinese emperor was a failure. In fact, he finally committed suicide in disappointment and frustration. It was only after his death that Shoki's spirit found its eternal vocation, as a tireless and indestructible smiter of demons in both his native land and Japan. His bearded visage, his glowering eyes, his flowing Chinese robes and his swirling, swishing sword have made him a familiar figure through several hundred years of Japanese art.

Shoki fighting a thunder god, represented by actor Nakamura Utayemon. Painted by Sadanobu Hasegawa in 1886, such "real-life" pieces were very popular with the public during the 19th century.

Their joyful reunion was interrupted by the sound of the demon's return. The daughter quickly hid her mother in a stone chest in the corner of the room, but such subterfuge could not fool the *oni* king. A plant in the garden sprouted one flower for every mortal present in these accursed precincts and the second bloom which betrayed the mother had been only too clear for him to see. So at any rate must it have proved had the bride not quickly offered her own alternative explanation: she was pregnant, she said, with his own child.

Overjoyed, the king ordered a celebration and soon he and his devil courtiers were in a stupor. While they snored, the women crept out past the still sleeping dogs. Then the priestess who had first helped the mother appeared again; she told them to take a boat and float downriver to safety.

Just when they seemed to have got away, however, they heard a commotion within the castle. The demons had awoken, hungover and desperate for water. Staggering bleary-eyed down to the riverbank, they all crouched down to quench their infernal thirst. So deeply did they drink that the current of the stream sucked the women's craft back towards the castle whence it had just come.

Fortunately, the priestess had a plan: to stand up, open their kimonos and expose themselves to the demons. The *oni* broke off their drinking at once, goggle-eyed and gaping at this exhibition. So uncontrollably did they giggle in prurient glee that they spewed back all the water they had drunk, and the bride and her mother were borne away on a mighty wave. Once more the *oni*'s evil had been outdone by virtuous cunning.

The Oni and the Priest

So it would turn out too in the story of the female *oni* and the young priest. The novice had often asked his superior if he could go out into the forest to gather nuts, but permission had always been refused. He persisted and was duly allowed so long as he took three charms with which he might keep the devils who infested the woods at bay.

Yet scarcely had the priest ventured into the trees than he was seized by an old *oni* woman. She imprisoned him and all night he lay in her house paralysed by fear, but with the morning light his spirits revived and soon he had a plan. He begged to go to the privy. His abductress was not so foolish as to let him leave her sight unsupervised, so she tied some cord to him and grasped the end firmly as she stood outside the door.

Once inside, he untied the cord and fastened it to a beam. Whispering to the first charm he had been given, he asked it to respond on his behalf when his captor called, then he exited through a window. Minutes later the crone asked what was holding him up. He would be done soon, a voice replied, if she would just wait. The devil-woman soon grew suspicious and upon pulling open the door she was enraged to see he was long gone.

Despite the headstart, she soon caught him up. The young priest hurled his second talisman to the ground and the *oni* found her way blocked by a mountain of sand. This slowed her, yet even so she quickly overhauled the escapee again. In desperation he hurled his last charm and a swift river sprang up in his pursuer's path which carried her off while he made his way to the temple and safety.

Hearing of his escapade, his mentor hid him in a box suspended from the ceiling. When the old *oni* turned up and demanded the youth, he was ready with a strategy. He would hand over the boy, he cunningly said, if she would oblige him by obeying certain simple instructions. She agreed, and asked him what it was that he wanted. First she must grow tall, he said – so she did, her head almost touching the temple roof. Next he asked her to grow small, and she duly shrank to the size of a bean. The old priest promptly popped her into his mouth and swallowed her, and let his digestive juices go to work. In due course his bowels moved, and he passed a swarm of buzzing flies!

These two figures are *koma inu* or temple guardians, protective lion-like dogs used to ward off evil spirits and bad luck. Wood sculptures, Kamakura period, 1185–1393.

The Tengu, *Irascible Trickster*

The *tengu* serves as the guardian deity of his area's mountains and their animals, plants and people, but he is also an inveterate mischief-maker whose stormy temperament means that his sense of humour deserts him the moment the joke is at his own expense.

In the mountains of Shimane region there once lived a good-for-nothing who idled in bed all day, emerging only at night to break into neighbours' homes or waylay travellers. One morning as he headed home through the pinewoods, he decided to take a break beside a remote wayside shrine.

Heedless of the sanctity of the spot, he made a fire and was just lighting up his pipe when he heard the strangest bird-cry. Looking up into a tree-top he saw what appeared to be a great bird with a long tail: he whipped out his gun, fired and it fell to the ground. Just as he was about to pick up his prize, however, the "bird" glared at him. To his horror he found he had shot a *tengu*.

Who did he think he was, the bird-man asked him angrily, to shoot at such a spirit? Unmoved by his pleas for forgiveness, the *tengu* touched his persecutor with a twig, whereupon the miscreant's body erupted into flames from top to toe. His screams shattered the dawn silence, and brought people running from the village. They found him rolling around on the forest floor in agony, fatally injured. He told them of his ill-fated encounter with the *tengu* and confessed all his previous crimes against his community. The villagers did their best to help him but his case was hopeless.

A legend like this is a reminder of the *tengu*'s origins as a local guardian deity. His rule might on occasion be ruthless – those who cut firewood without permission might well find their homes in flames – but he can still be seen as a sort of social and ecological spirit-policeman for his territory.

The Woodcutters and the Wens

Yet the *tengu*'s predominant role in Japanese tradition is essentially as a comic figure. The humour starts with his grotesque appearance – a combination of man and bird, with little feathered wings, claws and a long, bill-like proboscis. An expression of arrogant fury completes this unprepossessing picture, a bright red face underlining the impression of uncontrollable rage.

Although religious in its origins, the figure of the *tengu* clearly developed along satirical lines.

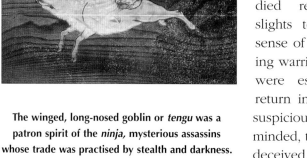

The winged, long-nosed goblin or *tengu* was a patron spirit of the *ninja*, mysterious assassins whose trade was practised by stealth and darkness. Votive painting, *c.*1800.

His touchy irascibility symbolized the absurd pointlessness of pomposity and pride. Traditionally *tengus* were held to be the reincarnations of those who had died resenting imagined slights to their overgrown sense of honour; overweening warriors and vain priests were especially likely to return in this form. Deeply suspicious and yet simpleminded, the *tengu* was easily deceived, as the tale about woodcutters and wens illustrates to great effect.

There were two woodcutters in a mountain village, as unlike one another in temperament as can be imagined; one was the cheeriest of souls, the other a curmudgeon. One thing they did have

The Trickster Tricked

The tengu's tricks often appear rough and ready to modern Western eyes, when, that is, they don't seem positively vicious. Strange knockings in the night; unaccountable breakages; draughts that blow from nowhere and lights without obvious source: the tengu's repertoire was reminiscent of the European poltergeist's.

Yet he thought nothing too of taking lives in terrible fires and hideous accidents – there was definitely a surly edge to the tengu's sense of humour. Any fun had at his expense would certainly have to be paid for dearly. One young man, a self-styled sceptic with a head full of Western ways, once scoffed at the superstitions of his rural neighbours. Clad in a feather cloak, in mocking impersonation of a tengu, he climbed a pine tree and screeched with delighted laughter as the cloddish peasants below bent down to do him homage. But the spirit of the mountain was not amused, and the youth's own laughter turned to screams as a sudden gust tore him from his lofty perch and dashed him down to his death.

Another lad too smart for his own good duped a tengu into trading his cloak of invisibility for a worthless twig. He was finally caught by the angry spirit and plunged into an icy river from which he barely escaped with his life.

in common, though, was a disfiguring facial wen, one man's on the right, the other's on the left. Late one afternoon the first woodcutter lost his way in the woods and was forced to shelter for the night in a hollow tree. As midnight approached, he was terrified to see that a troop of tengu had gathered on the ground before him to make merry.

As time went on his fear gave way to curiosity, and soon he was carousing with the best of them. The tengu said he must join them again sometime. He promised to return very soon, but was perplexed to find that his word was not adequate. They insisted on some surety for his bond and he stood by bewildered as they discussed what they should demand. To his amazement, they decided on the lump from his face. Rather than a blight, they had assumed it was a treasured possession. He could scarcely conceal his delight when they whipped it magically from his face. He could have it back, they told him sternly, when he returned in fulfilment of his bond. He renewed his vow gravely, then went home at dawn elated.

When the other woodcutter asked him enviously what doctor had rid him of his wen, he gave him a truthful account of what had happened. The other determined that he would go and have his own mark removed the same way.

That night, when the tengu returned to the site of their festivities, they were thrilled to find what they thought was their boon companion already waiting. He had kept his word, they said delightedly and he must have his precious lump back immediately. They were astounded when the woodcutter went off weeping into the night – his face was now doubly disfigured by large wens standing proud on either cheek.

111

Kappa, *the Water Vampire*

The *kappa* was one of the most sinister and malevolent spirits in Japanese mythology, yet it could also have benign, even protective, aspects and was considered to be a creature whose word could be trusted never to be broken.

Among the various wills, deeds and other documentation which enshrine the official existence of the Japanese family, some households have another paper whose origins are altogether more strange. Touring rural regions in the late 1950s, the Japanese-American folklorist Hiroko Ikeda was astonished when several families proudly produced written agreements which a spirit had signed. In these affidavits the *kappa*, or water vampire, swore to leave this particular family alone. It would refrain from further mischief towards them, it vowed, and even do its best to protect them from that moment forth. This is the paradox of the *kappa*: although in some ways the most dangerous of Japan's spirits, it is also the only one whose word might conceivably be believed.

Not that, in appearance or general behaviour, the *kappa* does much to encourage confidence. It has the build of a child, they say, yet the air of innocence stops abruptly there. Like the *oni*, the *kappa* will on occasion rape women – yet these victims might yet be thankful to escape with their lives. This is after all a being that lurks underwater in rivers, lakes or ponds, stealing forth to suck the blood of passing mortals, and livestock, through the anus. The distended anus of many a victim of drowning was widely attributed to its attentions. Where riverbanks and lakesides it frequented could not be avoided, travellers moved hastily to avoid falling victim themselves.

The *kappa*'s slimy (sometimes scaly) skin is a greenish-yellow colour; its fingers and toes are webbed; and its head is indented at the crown. A pool of liquid fills this concavity, which is said to be the source of the *kappa*'s strength. If spilled, it is immediately weakened, though causing this may be easier said than done, for the *kappa* has fear-

A *kappa* astride a cucumber on which it takes to the air like a dragonfly. This ape-cum-tortoise creature could be placated with an offering of the vegetable. Hokuga, *c.*1830.

some strength. Yet here too its paradoxical nature may once again come to the rescue, for it is said that some *kappas*, bowing politely to intended victims, have ended up draining away this precious fluid by their own action, allowing their fortunate quarry to escape. The truth is that, with all its wicked ways, the *kappa* has qualities of honour and integrity which other demonic beings would only scoff at – this makes it one of the most interesting, and least predictable, of Japanese spirits.

So it proved, for instance, with the *kappa* who emerged from its pond one day to attack a cow which an incautious farmer had tethered to a nearby tree. As it thrust its arm all the way up her innards in an attempt to reach the root of her tongue, the poor creature bellowed in pain and fear and attempted to flee. Confined as she was by her rope, however, she could only spiral round and round the tree trunk – but as she did so the *kappa* found itself trapped in its turn. Drawn by his animal's cries, the farmer came running, whereupon the *kappa* panicked, broke away and ran, leaving behind its arm, wound tightly to the tree by its victim's tether.

The farmer picked up his gory trophy and took it back home. Night after night the *kappa* pleaded outside the farmhouse for its return, but the man was implacable – until finally he agreed to restore it, so long as the *kappa* swore never to trouble him or his neighbours again. It was with the utmost reluctance that the spirit gave its word, but once given it would never be broken. From that time forth it left the local people and their stock alone. As for its arm, that was easily healed, for the *kappa* is famous for its skill in bone-setting, mending broken – even severed – limbs without deformity or scar.

One *kappa* less ugly than his kinsfolk was able to pass as a real child, and it was in this guise that he accosted those who passed the pond where he lived. Each person who approached was challenged to try his strength at "pull-finger", and, seeing no harm in indulging "the little boy", most would laughingly oblige. Their amusement would not last long, however, as, summoning its superhuman strength, the *kappa* quickly pulled its hapless victims down into the depths where it greedily sucked forth their lifeblood.

Soon the situation had grown intolerable and local villagers met to discuss what might be done. One man promised to rid them of their scourge so long as his lord would lend him a strong, swift horse. Thus mounted, he made his way down to the water's edge. There he met the "boy", and locking fingers as requested, the rider whipped his

horse fiercely and drove him on with cries. Taken by surprise, the *kappa* was caught off balance, and dragged along behind the galloping horse. The fluid spilled from the crown of its head and it was forced to beg its mortal abductor for mercy. If he let it go, the *kappa* said, it would teach him its bone-setting skills. His captor having agreed to what it asked, the *kappa* swore never to trouble the people again, and did indeed instruct its vanquisher in the art of bone-setting. Armed with this occult lore, the man was able to set up in medical practice, the founder of a dynasty of surgeons.

The apparent calm and tranquillity of a rural pond or lake is in stark contrast to the potential menace of any *kappa* which might be found residing there. Both humans and animals in the vicinity were at grave risk from a blood-sucking attack.

Spirits of the Storm

The countless islands of Japan receive a frequent buffeting from the weather which rolls in off the seas. Unsurprisingly, therefore, the violent sublimity of the storm and the seductive beauty of blanketing snow have found reflection in tales of majestic yet deadly passion.

Every year the seas around Japan are agitated by the autumn equinox's roaring storms. Wild ocean breakers batter the eastern coast, while even the sheltered western waters seethe like a boiling cauldron in which the hardiest fisherman fears to put to sea. Yet the most terrifying gales of all blow inland, across the waters of Lake Biwa. Lying in the lee of the Hira mountains, Japan's largest lake should be well sheltered, but the local microclimate creates special conditions. Scouring the wooded slopes above the lake, sweeping down to lash its calm waters into terrible waves, the "Hira Hurricane" returns every autumn, without fail. The trees bow down before its blast as if begging for mercy, but it rushes on, impervious to their pleas. There may be greater storms at sea, but none are more intimidating in destructive power or pathos.

Love and the Lighthouse-keeper

Such winds provide the fitting meteorological memorial to a tempestuous love and its tragic end, for it was at the lake that one of the greatest ever love stories was set, a tale of passion and rancour.

On the eastern shore, a lighthouse once stood to guide shipping safely round a rocky promontory. The lighthouse-keeper was a handsome, generous-spirited young man. One fine spring day a party from over the lake came to visit his lighthouse and among them was a fair young girl with whom he promptly fell in love. To his delight she returned his feelings, and was even ready to take the initiative – for his duties tied him to his home at night. Every night from then on, therefore, once her parents were safely asleep, the girl stole down to the waterside and set off in a boat for the other shore. On still nights the waters were smooth and her oarstrokes echoed loud in an uncanny silence; on others, her bucking boat seemed ever set to dash her down to her death in the waves. But she never feared, for there on the horizon the light of her lover shone, beckoning her ever onwards.

On into autumn she crossed the lake each night. The equinoctial gales blew up, but she never thought of missing a tryst – no storm could match the force of the feelings that surged in her heart. Yet once the first thrill of passion had passed, the lighthouse-keeper was beginning to find it all unsettling. Was it not unfeminine for her to take the initiative? Was there not something inhuman about anyone so heedless of the angry storm?

So it was that the girl's devotion came to count against her – her fidelity was evidence of her falseness; her heroism the sign of diabolical birth. So rattled had her lover become by her intensity that he concluded she was really a devil or dragon-girl. One night he decided to put his suspicions to the test and extinguished his beacon. A diabolical spirit would find its way to his side regardless; it never occurred to him what a mortal girl might do.

Out in a dark, moonless night, the girl could not believe her eyes when she emerged from a trough of waves to see only unrelieved blackness before her. Now directionless, deserted by the love which had guided her, she was thrown about helplessly. As her boat foundered and she was dragged under to her death, she concluded that her lover had been unfaithful and cursed him. The storm suddenly redoubled in its violence; mountainous waves went scudding across the lake, laying siege to the shore and smashing all before them. Perched alone on the rock, the lighthouse stood sentry on a grim front line, but by morning it had been washed away along with its young keeper.

Yuki-onna, the Snow Maiden

His snow coverlet drawn rudely aside by the searchers' shovels, the lost traveller was finally revealed, a smile of complete fulfilment on his face. Far from being buried in an icy grave, he had the air of one who had spent the wild night in living passion, enveloped in the arms of a beautiful mistress.

The agonies of frostbite forgotten, and his panic-stricken struggles stilled, a feeling of serenity stole over the hypothermia victim preparing him for the most seductive, the most deceptive of all deaths. This paradox was personified in the form of Yuki-onna, the Snow Maiden, who lured hapless men to her soft bed and her embrace. Her face a ghostly, ghastly white, she had the most beautiful body and the gentlest caress: no man could resist her advances – nor were many so fortunate as to survive them.

One young man who did fell in with Yuki-onna while travelling through the mountains with a much older companion. They were caught out by a blizzard and took refuge in a remote cabin.

Waking with a start in the deepest midnight, the youth saw a beautiful woman come into the room. She leaned over his sleeping companion, and breathed on his face. Then she stole across the floor to where the young man lay rigid with fear: she would spare him, she said, if he swore never to mention her visit to a living soul.

Next morning he found himself alone, the woman gone and his friend dead. Seized with terror, the young man went on and said nothing to anyone about what had happened. Years later he fell in love with a young woman named Yuki, a common enough name, even though it means "snow". They married, had children and lived happily.

One night as he saw her pale face reflecting the light of evening, he was reminded of that night in the mountain cabin so many years before. Amused at the thought, he told his young wife the whole strange story. Suddenly her appearance changed; there before him stood the Snow Maiden, her white face a mask of fury. Had he not solemnly promised, she demanded, to keep her secret? If she now spared him a second time, she went on, it was only for the sake of her beloved children; thereupon she melted away into the night, and was never seen by her family again.

Spectres of the Departed

Ghost stories abound in Japan, a mark of the continuity that is seen between this world and the next. During the Festival of the Dead the souls of the departed are believed to travel on ships called *shoryobuni*. The ocean is luminescent with the light the souls give off as they return to the spirit world. Mortal seamen dare not go near for fear their vessel will be sunk.

A novice monk in a Japanese temple once gathered all his closest friends about him for an evening's entertainment, swapping scary ghost stories in his room. When the tales had been told and all had been enjoyably affrighted, the guests took their leave and went their separate ways. Two young men, however, had come a greater distance than the others; they settled down where they were to pass the night on the novice's floor. A little later, one of them awoke and, staring into the darkness from his bed, saw a ghostly young woman stooping down to pick up the sleeping monk. Bed, bedding and all, she bore him effortlessly from the room; moments later she was back for his friend. Stunned as he was by the terrifying sight, the young man recovered himself sufficiently to scream for help, but none heard him and he lay there helpless and alone the whole night long.

Only when dawn finally broke did he feel able to stir from the spot where he lay. Pulling himself upright, he fled headlong into the cold morning air. Too terrified to speak of what he had seen, he attempted to resume his life in the world outside, but he found himself drawn back to the temple regularly, to pray that no further calamities should befall him.

A skeletal spectre sent by a demoness looms over two samurai warriors she wishes to torment. Print by Utagawa Kuniyoshi, 19th century.

On one of these visits, he happened to notice a young woman. She was there again on his next visit, and the two talked to one another. In time they were married. With her he found that happiness which had eluded him since the sinister disappearance of his friends. He thanked Heaven for sending him so virtuous and devoted a bride. He no longer felt any need to return to the temple; his life was back on an even keel at last. No harm could threaten him now.

As the years went by, he even forgot the anniversary of those uncanny events – until the evening he went into the kitchen unexpectedly and saw his wife bent over as she stoked the fire. The lurid light of the flames dancing on her face showed a different visage from the one he thought he knew: it was the face of the temple ghost!

As she turned to confront her stunned husband the spectre clearly knew that her secret was out. She advanced towards him across the floor with a malicious leer. Stretching out her arms in a mocking embrace she came up and breathed upon his blenching face. He fell away onto the kitchen floor, as if in a faint. When his servants found him, however, he was lying there quite dead; of his beloved wife, no sign was anywhere to be seen.

Ghost Mother

Death, in Japanese traditional culture, has never been the abrupt cut-off it has been in the modern West: the spirit lingers long after the bodily remains have been buried. Any loose ends which may need to be tied up, any important business left unfinished at the time of death; it will fall to the living ghost to bring all such matters to a clear conclusion. Until this is done, the spectre of the departed will be unable to depart. Instead it must walk the Earth, unsatisfied and restless. Unavenged resentments, unfulfilled vows or undischarged duties – all these living debts must be made good in death. No myth illustrates this more vividly than the tale of the ghostly mother.

A certain tradesman, the story goes, was about to shut up shop one evening, when a pallid and harassed-looking woman came rushing in; her hair was dishevelled and her manner furtive. She pointed wordlessly to his stock of *ame* – a nutritious syrup often given to babies – handed over her money and then rushed out with her purchase into the gathering darkness.

Although there was certainly something odd about her, the shopkeeper could not place it; he accordingly dismissed her from his mind and got on with the work in hand. The next evening, however, she came rushing in breathlessly once more; she was there again the following night, and the evening after. Since she always waited until his shop was deserted, none of his other customers ever saw her; nor, for that matter, did they know her by his description. His curiosity now thoroughly aroused, the shopkeeper determined to follow her home one evening. Some dark presentiment made him call on some friends as he

A ghost mother carries a figure of Jizo, whose various roles include guardian of the souls of dead children. *The Lantern of the Ghost of Sifigured Oiwa*, Edo Period, c.1852.

117

quietly pursued her. It was just as well, for the woman stopped at the temple graveyard, turned and went in at the gate. Their hearts beating clamorously now, the shopkeeper and his friends went tiptoeing after her. To their horror, they saw her lift a gravestone and step into the earth.

That shock was nothing, however, to that which they felt moments later when, drawing near to the tomb, they heard the sound of an infant crying inside. Bringing lights and equipment, they soon had the grave opened up. Within lay the shopkeeper's customer, a lifeless corpse. But on her lips was a smile of contentment, and in her arms lay a lusty child, tended by the loving mother who had died with him unborn. Finding herself dead and buried while the child still lived in her womb, the woman had known no other option than to bear and bring him up like any mortal mother. Now that she had succeeded in bringing her child to the attention of living carers who could rear him among mortals, the ghost mother could finally give him up to them, and surrender herself to the peace of the grave.

Ito and the Perfect Bride

Traffic back and forth between this existence and the afterlife was ceaseless, as the peculiar tale of Ito shows very well. One night a servant-girl came to summon him to an urgent meeting. His curiosity piqued, he went along unquestioningly. Far from his home she led him to the door of an abandoned-looking house in the woods; the door was opened and he was ushered courteously inside. Immediately he could see he was in the company of ghosts, yet so real did they seem, and so warmly did they speak to him, that he did not think to fear.

To his astonishment he found himself being introduced to a young lady – the daughter, his hosts said, of Shigehira. Now the famous Shigehira,

The Wife Who Returned

A certain young couple – O-Tei was the woman's name – were betrothed to be married: both longed to be united more than anything. But as is so often the way, the course of true love was crossed by misfortune, in this case by O-Tei's alarming decline in health.

Before their wedding could take place, her condition became critical: she had consumption, and it was clear she could not live for very much longer. Before she died she summoned her love to her, and told him that she must now leave, but she would return in a stronger body if he would only wait a while. Weeping, he gave her his word and when next day she died he repeated his heartfelt pledge in writing, burying the note in his beloved's grave.

The years of mourning went by and in time memories of O-Tei had become a little more faded. The young man's parents insisted that it was time for him to put his old love behind him; he was wasting his life this way.

So when they found him a prospective bride, he went along with the arrangement. He did indeed find happiness of sorts with this new wife, and with the child their love brought into being. His family was fated not to flourish, though. First the

young man's father and mother died; then, hardly had they gone than his wife and child were snatched from him. Reeling from this fourfold blow, the young man determined to travel, to escape from himself and the life he had been living.

And so it was that, some time later, he found himself in a remote village in a far-flung province he had never for a moment thought of visiting before. There was an oddly familiar look, he thought, about as Ito knew well, was a warrior of the Taira clan who had been executed by Yoritomo, vengeful chief of the Minamoto. These events, furthermore, had taken place six centuries earlier; the fair creature before him must have been dead for many generations. Her beauty and grace were such, however, that this seemed the most trifling of objections, and when it was suggested that the couple get married, he eagerly agreed.

There and then they were wed, and they spent a rapturous night together, the young man completely captivated by the charms of his bride. Just before dawn the time came for him to part, and, borne up as he was by the force of his love, Ito was unperturbed to be told that they were not to see each other again for ten years. For another such night, he said, he would wait a lifetime.

His words were to prove prophetic. From that time forth he visibly sickened and grew frail for all about him to see. Inwardly, however, he felt only

youth and vigour. He was empowered by his secret love. The years passed, and at last it was time for Ito to reunite with his lovely bride. He wondered how he was going to conceal his mounting excitement. He need not have worried, however: his physical vigour fading away apace, his mother was coming close to despair at her son's deterioration.

At last the evening came when the ghostly servant-girl appeared again. Before setting out with her, though, he insisted on speaking with his mother. Opening his heart, he told her of his wedding night a decade ago, and of the bliss he anticipated that night and for all time to come. As Ito thus brought his tale to its conclusion, his weeping mother saw him breathe his last, an expression of the utmost contentment on his gaunt features. She did not know whether to weep or rejoice. Had her son died in a delirious dream, or had he moved on to a life of rapture with his chosen lover?

the young woman who waited at his table in the inn. Even though he could swear that he had not met her before, she reminded him of the woman he had loved years ago.

When he asked her who she was, she told him she was his own O-Tei. The letter he had left in her grave had given her spirit comfort, she told him. Now she had returned to be with him as she had promised. Their love rekindled, the two wed again and enjoyed a long and blissful marriage.

Perhaps the most peculiar thing about this strange tale was that from that moment O-Tei lost every recollection of any life previous to the one she was living now.

The Boundlessness of Nature

Japan's moral fables and pleasing fantasies are enlivened by a veritable menagerie of animals. The serpent normally exudes an air of menace, while the fox often appears as an intermediary between the earthly plane and the spirit world. Meanwhile, a host of creatures respond to acts of human kindness and cruelty with appropriate rewards and punishments.

An old woman watched in horror one day as a naughty boy hurled a stone at a sparrow and broke its wing. As it fluttered about helplessly on the ground, she saw a crow circling hopefully overhead. She did not hesitate, but went over to the injured bird and put it in a box for safety.

As days went by she nursed it back to health, crooning over it and feeding it grains of rice. Her family could not believe the pains she was taking over such a lowly creature. But the kind-hearted woman had come to love her sparrow, and when its wing had healed, she fought to find the resolve to release it. She knew it was the right thing to do, however, and so she took it outside and threw it into the air. Would it remember her? she wondered, as it took its unsteady flight for freedom.

She moped for days, mourning the loss of her sparrow. Weeks later it returned, bearing in its beak a tiny seed which it dropped at her feet. She resolved to treasure the gift, and planted it out in the garden. Her family mocked, but they were left looking foolish when a trunklike vine grew quickly, festooned with gigantic gourds. There were enough not just for the woman and her family, but for the rest of the village besides – and that was by no means the limit of the sparrow's bounty. For, the glut of gourds being overwhelming, with far too much fruit to go round, the old woman hung eight of the largest up to dry.

The tale involving a sparrow and gourds was a parable about greed and jealousy. A gourd-shaped vase, from southern Kyushu, 19th century.

She had reasoned that they would make ideal containers for storage, but when the time came to open them up and hollow out their insides, she found that they were already fulfilling that role. Although supposedly dry and husky, their weight was absolutely incredible, and it was with mounting excitement that the old woman cut the lid off the first. From within spilled fine white rice in the most perfect, shapely grains – and the more she poured, the more came flowing inexhaustibly from within.

With seven more endless fountains of grain at their disposal, her family's future was assured: from being among the poorest, they were now the richest folk for many miles around. But while most of their neighbours rejoiced with them, there was still somebody prepared to cast an envious eye. An old woman who begrudged her neighbour's blessing did not see why she too should not be blessed: she would win the same favour for herself, she determined, whatever it took. And so, having heard the story of the sparrow, she knew just how to proceed: taking sharp stones, she let fly at the birds in her yard.

It took her several attempts, but in time she succeeded in knocking one sparrow over and stunning it. Eagerly, she picked it up and snapped its wing. One would not be enough to assure the sort of fortune she was envisaging, so she did not rest until she had injured several more.

Then, tossing them scraps of food and urging them to get a move on and start making her fortune, she hectored them back to health. They could not wait to get away from her house and from her cold "care". A few weeks later, they all returned, each with a seed in its beak. Delighted, the old woman planted them in the ground. When her vine had grown, however, it turned out to yield more bitter fruit: from her gourds spilled plagues, pests, sores and all manner of misfortune.

Tales of Turtles

Kindness to animals is always amply repaid, as is shown by two stories about turtles spared by fishermen who found them in their nets.

A year or more after such an act of generosity Fujiwara no Yamakage was crossing the sea in his vessel, with his wife and beloved son following in another. His son was actually the fruit of his late first wife, but the boy was shown such affection by his stepmother that it never occurred to Fujiwara to doubt her. Unbeknown to her trusting husband, however, she had been plotting murder and during the voyage she saw her opportunity. Throwing the child overboard at night, she waited a while before raising the alarm. By the time the convoy had come around and the search had started there was no trace of the boy to be found.

Yamakage wept with joy when a turtle appeared, bearing the boy on its shell back. His wife wept too, but her tears were of rage and frustration. That night the turtle came to Yamakage in a dream and warned him of his wife's duplicity. Once safely ashore, the merchant sent his son to a monastery, well away from her attentions.

In another story kind Urashima spared a turtle's life and saw his catch turn into a beautiful bride before his very eyes. Returning with him to the turtle kingdom, she introduced him to a life of pleasure and ease in an undersea paradise.

But it seems to be man's nature to be discontented, even in paradise itself, and it was not long before Urashima was pining for his humble home and his impoverished parents. His wife

The Feminine Fox

In Japan the fox or kitsune stands for female wiles. The sleek beauty and sumptuous fur of the animal underlines this association, its brush calling to mind a woman's long tresses.

In Japanese mythology many an unfortunate man finds himself seduced by a sly fox in a woman's form; sometimes he even marries a vixen. Women too may fall victim to the fox, though it possesses them not as a mortal man but a spirit lover – control by a fox spirit is thought to be a cause of mental illness.

Yet Western readers may overestimate the fox's sexual symbolism. The motivations of the animal's trickery are more complex and obscure. While the sexual overtones are undeniable, they are frequently inadequate to the facts of the tale. At times the fox may only be after food, at others it may be motivated by mischief for the sheer sake of it. In some tales the fox appears in another guise entirely, not as a trickster at all but as a conscientious messenger between divinities and mortals.

A Strange Bewitching by Foxes, by Utagawa Kuniyoshi, woodblock print, c.1845.

Sinuous Serpents and Dragons

In common with most mythological traditions around the world, an impressive array of snakes wriggle and writhe their way through Japan's ancient tales, representing primitive evil and lust.

Feelings regarded as improper or "unnatural" tend to find representation in this symbol, which is why the snake turns up so often in myths of ungoverned female desire, despite what might seem to be its obvious male form. Hence in one tale a girl who burns with unlicensed love for a young man of her acquaintance is turned into a huge snake, which then pursues its hapless victim.

Yet there is much more to the snake than sexual symbolism: it is also strongly associated with water. A form of primal energy, the sinuous coilings of the snake call vividly to mind the endless movement of a flowing stream, an impression which is only reinforced by its real-life taste for watery habitats.

The dragon – little more than a giant snake with wings – is seen, like its earthbound relation, as a water spirit, albeit one whose presence is discerned in mighty clouds of vapour and lashing rainstorms. This identification with water may seem odd, but it is derived from the long-standing Chinese tradition of dragons as guardians of lakes and rivers.

Yegara-no-Heida killing the giant serpent Uwabami, said to be capable of eating a man on horseback whole. Woodblock by Kuniyoshi, *c.*1830.

begged him to abide by the choice he had made, but in time she reluctantly allowed him to make his return. She gave him a little box to carry with him; the moment he wished to come back he was to squeeze it, but on no account must he open it. She bade him a sad farewell, and he immediately found himself upon his native shore.

There was no sign of his family anywhere to be seen. Asking around among the people he saw, he told them who he was, but they insisted that the only Urashima they had heard of had vanished into the ocean 300 years before. In his shock, he grabbed involuntarily at his casket and, without thinking, he flipped it open, realizing his error as he did so. The voice of his wife came to him over the waves, calling out reproachfully: he had broken his word and he could never join her in her world again. So it was that Urashima found himself adrift both in place and time, exiled from his new home and marooned in another age.

The Grateful Crab

Close as relations between animals and humans may be in such stories, they can be even closer still in tales of intermarriage. The story about the grateful crab sets two tales of animal gratitude together, first to upset, and then to re-establish the normal rules and regulations.

The story starts with a kindly girl buying a crab from a fisherman and letting it go. Her father, meanwhile, every bit as compassionate – if a little incautious – was attempting to prise a frog from the jaws of a hungry snake. So tightly did the serpent grip its catch, that try as he might he could not release it. Finally, in a moment's madness, he made the snake a promise: if it freed the frog, he told it, it could have his daughter's hand in marriage. The snake complied, but looked him firmly in the eye before slithering way.

That night a man came to the father's door to claim the fulfilment of his promise. It had to be the snake, he knew, and he asked him to return in a few days' time. The man agreed, but assured him that he would indeed be back to claim what he

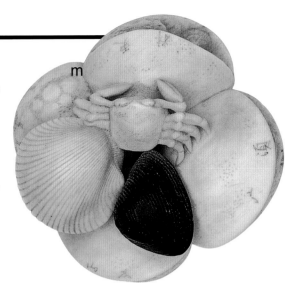

Crabs provided a not uncommon decorative motif in Japan, at times being associated with the souls of clan dead. Crab and seashell netsuke, 19th century.

believed was rightfully his. The father had no alternative but to explain to his daughter what he had promised. The poor girl took to her bed, and would not come out for anything. How was she to submit herself to such a monster?

Time went by inexorably, however, and a few nights later the snake returned in its reptilian form. Why should it pretend, when – man or snake – it had been made a promise? Although the father tried to bar its way, the snake simply glided past him to the daughter's room. It hammered on the door with its tail as she cowered within. But help was at hand – the gods to whom she prayed could not disregard the pleas of one who had shown such generosity herself.

From outside, a murmuring crescendo could soon be heard. As the noise grew and grew, the girl's father peered incredulously from his door at the army of crabs which came sidling across the shingle, filling the night with the noise of 1,000 scrabbling claws. He backed away in bewilderment and terror as the advancing columns came pouring in though his open door. On through the house they marched to the chamber where the snake was making ready to deflower its unwilling bride. Swarming all over the astonished serpent, they engulfed it completely in a seething mass of snapping, snipping claws. Within seconds it was cut to ribbons; the girl who had saved the crab had herself been saved. In so doing, a benign love between fellow-creatures had prevailed over bestial, animalistic desire.

123

The Lives of Plants and Trees

A host of stories testify to the vital part played by flora in Japanese mythology; they have living, feeling souls in this tradition, just as humans and animals do. Even bonds of love were said to have existed between people and their many plants and trees.

The unrelenting noise of traffic besieges Tokyo's Hibiya Park from every side. Yet here in the shadow of the skyscrapers, and a mere stone's throw from the neon lights of Ginza, a refuge of sorts is to be had from the hubbub of metropolitan Japan. In the park's famous flower shop the most beautiful bouquets may be bought, their vivid colours banishing for an instant the drab duns of urban concrete all around. Even so, standing here at the heart of the city, it is hard to imagine that the elderly gingko or maidenhair tree at the centre of the park was once the tallest thing around. Whether found in their more natural, rural setting or dwarfed by their urban surroundings, trees remain an important symbol in Japan. The Hibiya ginko may seem marooned amid so much modernity, but its roots thrust deep into the mythic past.

The gingko tree has a very special significance in Japanese tradition. It was believed to be capable of loyalty, and strange overgrowths on its trunk and boughs were likened to a woman's breasts. In antiquity, it is thought, nursing mothers worshipped the tree for this latter reason, and the association has endured into the modern age.

When Hibiya was first developed it seemed appropriate to retain the sacred gingko tree as the natural centrepiece of the park. To the landscapers' consternation, however, the tree seemed to resent the development: it began to wither and refused to thrive. Gardeners from all around were called in to offer their advice, but in vain. The gingko's condition deteriorated; it seemed as though it wanted to die.

One twilight at the end of another day's work, the head-gardener was standing by the withered tree, shaking his head sadly as he wondered whether, even at this late hour, anything might yet be done to save it. Suddenly he became aware of the presence of an old woman standing beside him. She smiled as he started, and told him not to be alarmed. Had he not considered, she gently prompted, the tree's traditional associations? He might try irrigating its roots with milk and then see how it fared. Before he could answer, the old woman disappeared, and he was left standing open-mouthed. He did just as she had advised, however, and the gingko began to recover its old vigour at once.

Milk-white porcelain provided a perfect ground for auspicious motifs. Lotuses symbolized the afterlife. Kakiemon ware, 17th century.

The Glories of Nature

Japan's countless exquisite gardens are a testament to its people's love of the sheer beauty of trees, shrubs and flowers. The tending of such plants is seen as a sacred duty, their destruction as a barbaric act, while kindness to plants tends to be rewarded in myth, just as kindness to animals is.

Hence the tale of the man whose ravishing garden was the talk of the city of Kyoto. Apart from his aged mother, his plants were his only companions, and he regarded his flowers as his

The Great Chestnut of Kurita

While many myths concern particular species and relate to what may well have been real trees, some sound far too outlandish ever to have existed: the truth of these tales can only be symbolic.

The story of the oak of Tsukushi, for example, so tall that it cast a shadow across hundreds of kilometres, starts to make sense only in its end, where the tree falls down and measures its length on the ground.

As long as a mountain-range and wide enough for hundreds of people to walk on it side by side, its story seems to have been dreamed up to explain the existence of a rich seam of coal.

The significance of another giant tree, the great chestnut of Kurita, in Omi region, is to teach a moral. So tall was this tree that its shadow darkened the rice fields of many districts, and at last the provincial governor ordered that it should be chopped down.

Try as they might, though, his men could not fell it, for all the cuts they made in its trunk by day were mysteriously mended the next morning, forcing them to start again from scratch.

The other plants of the region honoured the tree as their king and lent their own balm each night to heal it – and by such ecological solidarity they seemed to be winning the war. But a moment of pride proved the tree's undoing: when one night the ivy offered its balm to

treat its wounds, it haughtily rejected the help of such a lowly creeper. Deeply offended, the ivy determined to be avenged. It went straight to the woodcutters in a dream and told them why

their work was being frustrated. Not only that, but it taught them how to prevent the other plants' healing from taking effect. Within a few days the mighty chestnut was felled.

Once its secret was revealed, the vast chestnut was brought crashing down.

friends. Their care was his duty and his joy, and he lived happy in these simple satisfactions. But the idyll could not go on for ever, and the eventual death of his mother came as a body blow. He was plunged into a deep depression from whose shadow he could see no prospect of ever emerging. Even his flowers now caused him sadness, when he considered that come wintertime they too would be dead. Their beauty could not endure, he saw – they would fade and die like all in this wretched world. As the light of day disappears with the dark of nightfall, so surely must all the life, all the beauty of the Earth pass away. No store was to be set by the things of this existence; he would leave this life behind and become a hermit in the Buddhist tradition.

Accordingly he left Kyoto and went to live in the mountains, where he gave his days over to quiet contemplation and prayer. No one came near his cell, nor did he seek for human company; indeed, many months went by in which he did not hear another voice. One evening, however, there came a diffident knocking at his door. He opened it to an elderly lady, dressed from head to foot in robes of the deepest blue. She begged him, in his sanctity and wisdom, to instruct her in the ways of the Buddha. Word of his holiness had travelled far, she said; he surely could not refuse her this boon.

He had never seen himself as a teacher, of course – indeed it was in flight from human company that he had first come here. Yet his visitor's request for education had been so pressing, he did not feel he could reasonably decline; such an old lady, in addition, could hardly be a threat to his priestly peace of mind.

He therefore ushered her inside and began his sermon. He had not been speaking long when a much younger lady walked in, clad all in green. She sat down beside the first visitor, and listened attentively as he preached. As the minutes went by the congregation swelled, as more ladies appeared in turn: one wore yellow, another white and pink, still another purple and red. Soon some thirty women were gathered there before him, but the hermit preached on gamely. His hearers smiled especially appreciatively as he emphasized the value of the lives of plants and animals as well as those of men.

His discourse over, the women gathered round and thanked him. They were in fact his flowers, they told him then, and they had come all the way from Kyoto to support him in his spiritual quest. Each in turn placed a little prayer-poem before him, then vanished into the chill night air. As the last one left, the dawn sun arose on the most beautiful morning he had ever seen. Dew-drenched leaves shone and sparkled in a vibrant symphony of silvered green; flowers of every conceivable colour added shimmering grace notes to this verdant theme. Birds sang their thanks for the glories of creation, while a little brook babbled happily along. Never, the hermit realized, had he known such happiness or such peace of mind.

Bonds of Love

The tale involving Akoya, accomplished daughter of a provincial governor in the reign of Emperor Mommu more than 1,200 years ago, is also one of love between people, plants and trees.

Akoya sat out one autumn evening with her *koto* (a Japanese long zither); soon, blending with her song, she heard the strains of a flute, enchantingly played, and she looked up to see a noble-looking young man in a gown of green. The two set down their instruments then and engaged in conversation. Before too long they were in love.

Every evening thereafter they met, but one night Akoya found her lover looking sad. This was the last time he might meet her, he said; he was destined to die the next day. Thereupon he vanished, and on the spot where he had been only the shadow of a pine tree could be seen.

Next day, woodcutters felled a great pine to provide timber for a new bridge, the river in flood having destroyed the old one. Once it was lying on the ground, however, they found themselves unable to shift it, however hard they tried, and however many men they used. At last Akoya heard of their difficulties and worked out that the fallen pine was her lost lover. Hurrying to the spot where the tree lay, she laid a loving hand upon it; the pine slid easily now, wherever she asked it to go.

Yet the associations of plants and flowers are not always so happy. In one tale the susuki grass was a young prince, handsome and brave. He fell in love with Yaye-zakura, loveliest of the cherry trees. For a time she resisted his earnest advances, but eventually she submitted to his green embrace. But their love-idyll was to be rudely interrupted by the jealousy of Ume, the Japanese plum tree.

Ume had loved Yaye-zakura long and vainly, and could not abide seeing her so rapturously entwined in another's leaves. Not only that, but in yielding to the susuki, she had fallen not for another tree but for a lowly grass. Roused by his speeches of outrage, all the trees rallied to his banner of war; the other grasses flocked to the side of Susuki and the most fearful of battles ensued.

Fiercely the two sides fought, the conflict as implacable as any ever contested by men; several times the trees were forced back and it seemed as though the grasses must finally carry the day. But when Kusu-no-ki, the camphor tree, arrived in the field, the tide of battle finally turned; he set the grasses alight and they burned down in their black-ened droves. Susuki fell, fighting bravely to the last, and his lover was left inconsolable. Just as cherry trees ever since have shed their blossom, so Yaye-zakura shaved her hair, lost her beautiful blossom and donned a nun's robes of dull black bark.

Hermits found inspiration in the glories of nature and 19th-century Edo-period paintings reproduced their beauty too, taking care to bring out their symbolism. These egrets wade in a stream by an island of irises, identified with summer; peacocks were auspicious, representing beauty and plenty.

127

Holy Man of Buddha

Many of the most appealing Japanese stories concern the country's great Buddhist saints. Wandering preachers such as En-no-Shokaku and Nichiren feature prominently, but the best known of all the many followers of Buddha was Kobo Daishi.

A young woman was working at her weaving one afternoon when she heard a diffident knock upon her door. Opening it, she found an old man, grimy and footsore from the road. In tones of the utmost politeness, he asked if he might have a little water. It was with some embarrassment that she told him her pail was dry. The nearest supply was some distance off, but he should not think of going himself. He should sit and rest while she went.

The wayfarer gratefully accepted and sat down to wait while the woman set off up the hillside. It was some time before she returned; tears brimmed in the old man's eyes, so touched was he by the pains she had taken on his behalf. But she laughed off his thanks. It had been no trouble at all; how could she have done less for any traveller?

The old man prepared to take his leave, but, before he resumed his journey, he told the woman he wanted to do something in return. Taking his staff, he struck the earth and a spring bubbled up right by her door. Never again, he said, would she have to undertake another such labour. With this the old man went on his way, leaving his hostess exclaiming in excitement.

Her neighbours flocked round to marvel at the old man's work. Where once had been only dry dirt, crystal-clear water now came gushing forth. Life, they realized, would never be the same old grind again. Some ran out to add their own thanks, but though they looked up and down the highway the old man was nowhere to be seen. Only then did it dawn upon them that they must

have received a visit from Kobo Daishi, the most celebrated saint of Buddhist Japan (also known as Kukai, founder of Shingon or "True Word").

A well-loved figure in Japanese folklore, Kobo Daishi is the subject of numerous stories and many are the wells which are attributed to his holy hand. Wandering incognito the length and breadth of the land, Kobo Daishi rewarded generosity wherever he went, but he punished mean-spiritedness. Hence the tale of the householder who refused him a few potatoes, on the pretext that they were too hard to think of giving to a guest. Kobo Daishi ensured that from that time on they would be. However long the man cooked his potatoes after that, they remained rock solid and impossible to eat – a fit diet for someone with such a stony heart.

And if Kobo Daishi could endow springs he could also take them away, as in the famous case of the village where the saint was refused water, and the water then neglected to flow. Upstream and downstream of that spot, the river ran on just as before – only at the village itself the stream had disappeared underground.

The special sanctity of Kobo Daishi was apparent from the very first; he was born, it is said, with his hands joined in prayer. The growing boy shone in every accomplishment, but he was most remarkable for his sanctity. His first sermons were offered on the southerly island of Shikoku which was his home, and there it was that the youthful saint worked his first miracle. A fox spirit seeking to deceive him, he drove all foxes from the island. After that he would rid many places of pests, from mosquitoes to fearful dragons.

Once, his meditations were interrupted by sea monsters. He chased them back into the sea by chanting mystic injunctions and by spitting in their faces – beams of light from the evening star had entered his mouth, endowing his saliva with special powers. Walking through a mountain pass one day, Kobo Daishi found some children weeping beneath a giant chestnut tree. They wanted nuts, but could neither reach the lower boughs nor climb the massive trunk. The saint accordingly instructed the district's chestnut trees to start bearing nuts from a very young age; even the smallest saplings were festooned in fruit from that time on.

The Power of the Sutras

The power of words over humankind has been remarked upon in every place, every time and in every culture. Some texts, however, may have such mystic force that they transcend any earthly meaning.

So it is, in Japan, with the sutras, as they have been recited down many centuries. The scriptures of Japanese Buddhism, these prayers have come down through tradition in their original Chinese and Sanskrit, but while only an elite may apprehend their meaning, their divine poetry is appreciated by all.

Holiest of all – so sacred indeed, that its mere title may be chanted in solemn prayer – is the famous Hokkeiyo or *Lotus*

Sutra, which claims to have been first preached by the Buddha himself on Vulture Peak in far-off India. Many mountains in Japan have inherited the Chinese version of this name, and the sutra itself recurs in myth as a symbol – almost as a character – in its own right. That few understand what it has to say does nothing to dull this scripture's power, or the devotion which the Japanese have always felt towards it.

In one story, for example, a saint commits a crime just to have the opportunity of being flung in jail so that he might bring the power of the *Lotus Sutra* to the other prisoners. In another the very flames of hell die down at the sutra's sound. The list of miracles wrought by its recitation is endless.

The elaborate frontispiece of the *Greater Sutra of the Perfection of Wisdom*, produced in the 14th century.

Mystics of the Mountains

Although never formally established in Japan, Chinese Daoism nonetheless had a great influence there. The concept of the mystic sage, a semi-immortal endowed with supernatural powers, took root in the Buddhist form of the *sennin* or mountain recluse.

Unaccustomed to the stress and ignominy of brute labour, the spirits grunted with exertion and pain as they set to shifting all too substantial mounds of rock and earth. Gods and demons, ghosts and goblins were marshalled here like so many coolie gangs. Spirits accustomed to tyrannize and terrify were instead reduced to the rank of slaves.

Yet while they rolled their eyes in disbelief at their sudden subjection and shook their fists aloft in their transports of rage, any rebellious thoughts they might be harbouring were quickly quelled by the overseer's stare. For high up in the rocks above the ravine where they were toiling stood the man who had set them to work – a meek and pious-looking individual with no hint of the heroic about him. And yet, if you looked more closely, there were signs of steeliness behind his mild gaze.

His conscript labour force had good reason to know this well. Had not one of their number, a fearsome ogre, refused to work as he had been required on the great rocky bridge the holy man was building from one mountain to another? And had he not ended up, for his pains, being immured in his own cave, with the promise that he would remain penned there for all time to come? No sensible spirit would make the mistake of underestimating this slight-looking figure, for this was En-no-Ozuna, or Gyoja, the "Ascetic Master".

Gyoja was one of a growing band of hermits who, during the chaotic years of fourteenth-century Japan, had turned their backs on society and headed for the peace of the mountains where they could think and pray. These holy men came to be revered as semi-immortals, transcending worldly concerns. Magic powers were attributed to them.

Some of the best-known Japanese *sennin* were imported from Chinese mythology. Typical of these was Tobo-Saku, "Prime Man of the East", a sage who remained frozen in time, never growing any older than he already was. He bore a peach in his hand, which replenished itself each year, forever fresh and young. Tobo-Saku symbolized the regenerative power of spring – just like the eternally young and beautiful Weiwobo, the "Queen Mother", who in Chinese lore was Xi Wang Mu, Queen Mother of the West.

Some *sennin* are closely associated with particular animals or plants; hence Rafu-sen is always thought of in connection with the fragrant plum-blossom through whose groves she nightly wandered. Kinko Sennin, "High Man With a Harp",

A *stupa* is both a Buddhist shrine mound and a receptacle for prayers. These wooden *stupas* form part of a massive collection of one million such objects known as the Hyakuman To, commissioned by a grateful Empress Shotoku following her defeat of an 8th-century rebellion.

Mountain settings were the norm for stories involving *sennin* and were usually associated with mysterious powers. The tale of Ikkaku reveals both the extent and limits of his abilities, as well as the crucial importance of dragons as suppliers of the life-giving rains. *Night Rain on Oyama*, woodcut by Utagawa Toyoshige, *c.*1830.

rides on the back of a crane as he strums, while Kiku-jido, "Chrysanthemum Grace-boy", never strays far from his special flower. Masters of all manner of supernatural feats, *sennin* fly through the sky and walk upon the waves, conjure spirits out of nowhere and appear and disappear at will. They may once have been based on real human hermits, but their myths left these mundane origins far behind, just as the holy men themselves had learned to rise above earthbound concerns.

Yet these figures had been born mortal and could never be fully otherwise. High as they might soar, they were always in danger of falling. A *sennin*'s supernatural powers could be lost if he allowed himself to be tempted by worldly desires; he would then come tumbling back down to earth. Not that this was necessarily the most tragic of fates, as the tale of Kume-no-Sennin shows.

He fell to earth after he had allowed his gaze to linger on the feet of a woman he saw washing clothes in a stream. Picking himself up, he cheerfully waved his status goodbye, leaving too his potential place in the pantheon of mythic glory. Instead, he wooed and wed his lovely laundress, to live happily – if obscurely – with her ever after.

The tragic fall of Ikkaku, the "single-horned" *sennin*, was also in some ways a blessing in disguise, for in his virtuous zeal he had rounded up and imprisoned all Japan's marauding dragons. While this may have brought a welcome end to their depredations, he failed to see that it also meant an end to the rain, for the clouds and the showers were in the dragons' keeping.

As crops dried up and the people despaired, men called in vain on Ikkaku for help – he was deafened by his fanaticism. Finally the ruler of the region hit upon a trick to set the dragons free. Finding the fairest lady he could at court, he sent her off to disport herself outside the *sennin*'s hermitage. Unable to resist, the not-so-holy man came out of his cave to gaze. So beguiled was he that he allowed himself to be pressed into accepting a goblet of sake. Doubly intoxicated by the force of alcohol and feminine caresses, he fell into her embrace oblivious as his powers ebbed away. Breaking out from their confinement, the dragons poured forth to fill the sky with billowing clouds. Before Ikkaku could shake off his languor, the heavens had opened and the gasping earth had been inundated with life-restoring rain.

131

THE SACRED SPIRIT OF GARDENS

Gardens, or *teien*, and the cultivation of plants and flowers are very ancient arts in Japan, offering the practitioner the means to create a visual, spiritual and psychological impression of the harmony and totality evident in nature through its five elements of river, sea, mountain, forest and field. These essentially Shinto beliefs were, in time, influenced by Buddhist notions of paradises, particularly mountainous ones, as places where one could attain a higher level of contemplation. Over time, a number of horticultural specializations emerged in Japan – including *ikebana* or flower arrangement and *bonsai* miniaturization – but underlying all, whether adorning imperial, noble, shrine or park settings, is the inspiring and manifest nature of the *kami* of the natural world. A mixture of trees and foliage, shrubs, moss, rocks, ponds, waterfalls, streams, bridges and gravel can be used in a myriad of aesthetic forms to create very different moods and spirits, from the ornate and highly sensual to the ideal of simple, unpretentious rustic beauty known as *wabi* ("cultivated poverty").

Above: Saiho-Ji Temple's moss garden was designed in the 14th century. The stone lanterns or *ishi-doro* offer reminders of the Buddhist mountain paradise as well as a functional base for moss to grow on.

Below: The austere garden was a Zen Buddhist development meant to foster contemplation and understanding. Rocks represent mountains and stones symbolize the endlessly repeated patterns of the sea.

Below right: Pine trees, camellia, plum blossoms and mountains adorn this large, mid-17th century *chatsubo* or storage jar for tea leaves. Zen monks drank tea to maintain their alertness during garden meditations.

Left: Sacred koi and lilies adorn a lake in the gardens at Rinno-Ji Temple in Sendai Honshu, forming part of the complex of buildings at the Toshogu Shrine. Use of water was particularly favoured by the nobility during the Heian period.

Below: A long-sleeved silk *furisode* garment worn on special occasions by children and young women. The embroidered design is of scenes of natural beauty, revered for their auspicious meanings and *kami*. Pine and maple trees occupy the upper half of the scene, while peacocks and peonies, symbolizing beauty and plenty, decorate the bottom. Running water courses throughout the piece. The intricacy and skill suggest the wearer was a member of the samurai class. Edo period, 19th century.

THE LEGACY OF JAPANESE MYTH

Maybe no other country's myths are so closely entwined into the fabric of public life as Japan's. The gods and spirits – the *kami* – they portray became objects of veneration early on, and, almost uniquely, they have remained so to the present. Over the centuries the worship of these many beings came together in the widely espoused Shinto religion.

At first Shinto seems to have been little more than a portmanteau noun to describe collectively the acts of worship that went on at the shrines of individual *kami*. Under official patronage, though, the cult of Amaterasu and the other divinities of the imperial clan gradually rose to prominence as the focus of national worship.

Even so, Shintoism remained a largely local, fairly disorganized religion until the middle of the nineteenth century. That changed after 1868, when the radicals who seized control at that time came to an extraordinary decision. While seeking to modernize the nation by adopting Western ideas, they concurrently looked backwards for their guiding ideology to the most ancient roots of Japan's history. Shinto, which over the preceding centuries had been largely overshadowed by Buddhism in the nation's spiritual life, now found itself in the position of something resembling a state religion.

An Imperial Cult

The advent of State Shinto, as it would become known, was intimately linked with the cult of the emperor. For much of Japanese history, the country's nominal head had been just that: a ruler only in name, conducting rites for the nation as a sort of high priest of Shintoism but exercising little if any real power. Under the Meiji reforms, he continued to have little to do with the day-to-day business of government, but became the focus of an intense cult as the living incarnation of Japanese nationhood. And beneath the whole elaborate structure of emperor-worship lay an infrastructure of myth that had its roots in the *Kojiki*, originally written down 1,150 years previously.

In the years after 1868, the divinity of the emperor – previously accepted in an abstract way – became a central tenet of state ideology. Children were taught in school that he was a direct descendant of Amaterasu; they learned, too, that the nation's history began in 660BC with the legendary Emperor Jimmu, the great-great-great-grandson of the sun goddess. While most patriotic

Emperor Akihito attending the annual rituals at Ise, still presided over by the ruler as the direct descendant of Amaterasu.

Japanese were happy to accept this version of events, extreme nationalists went further, claiming that the divine descent made the Japanese distinct from all other peoples – they were the "children of the gods". In the 1930s, such claims were to be used to justify imperialism on the grounds that foreign nationals were intrinsically inferior.

The adoption of State Shintoism had other effects on the balance of faiths in Japan, besides encouraging a new literalness in the interpretation of myth. While major temples flourished, receiving public financial support for the first time ever, many smaller shrines were adversely affected, seeing their local following co-opted by the national centres of worship. Meanwhile Buddhism, which had been the dominant religion in Tokugawa times, found itself relegated to a subordinate position. Under the policy known as *shinbutsu bunri* – separating *kami* and buddhas – Shinto shrines were purged of Buddhist imagery and many statues were destroyed.

The nationalist interpretation of Shinto rose to a frenzied climax in 1945, when young pilots, dedicating their lives to emperor and sun goddess, flew to their deaths on *kamikaze* missions, so

Colourful carp banners flutter in the breeze during _Tango-no-sekku_ or Boys' Day, held every May. The ancient symbol of the carp – persevering and tenacious – is particularly dominant on this day when the mythic heroes are celebrated as role models and boys are motivated to become spirited and healthy.

called in memory of the wind sent by the *kami* six centuries earlier to drive back Mongol invaders of the homeland. Then, with the Allied victory, it too came crashing down in flames.

Japan's post-war constitution, imposed by the occupying powers, took pains to separate church and state: Article 20 specified that "no religious organization shall receive any privileges from the State, nor exercise any political authority". As a consequence, Shinto shrines lost their financial support and had to revert to the earlier tradition of living off the contributions of believers. Freedom of religion was guaranteed, and other religions including Buddhism and Christianity were actively encouraged. And, crucially, Emperor Hirohito agreed to make a radio broadcast to the nation in which he formally renounced any claim to divinity. In future he was to reign not as a god but as a constitutional monarch.

The effects of these momentous changes on Japanese attitudes to Shinto – and thus the national heritage of myth – have been subtle but profound. In some respects, religious life has returned to a pre-Meiji pattern, with local shrines regaining their place as spiritual focal-points for neighbourhood communities. The old, syncretist approach to religion has also revived. In opinion polls, over 90 per cent of the population still describe themselves as followers of Shinto, while 75 per cent call themselves Buddhists – indicating that most see no contradiction in acknowledging both faiths.

In fact the two complement each other well, as they have done through history. Shinto continues to be the religion of choice for celebrating such life-oriented events as births and marriages and also for the blessing of new enterprises, be they construction projects or start-up businesses. But Buddhist rites are usually preferred for the burial of the dead.

The two faiths also happily co-exist in many Japanese homes, where a Buddhist altar can often be found alongside a Shinto "god-shelf", so called from the many amulets, tokens and other symbols of the deities displayed upon it. Selling such objects, reckoned to promote good health as well as success in exams, driving tests, career moves and other imponderables, is an important fundraiser for many shrines. Shinto priests also raise money by blessing new buildings or business ventures. One shrine near Tokyo even specializes in the benediction of new cars, taken there by owners eager to avert garage bills and accidents.

A Conservative Tradition

In other respects, the legacy of Shinto is less benevolent. From such incidents in the myths as Izanagi's descent to the underworld (see page 36) and Susano's defiling of Amaterasu's weaving hall with the hide of a dead pony (see page 40), the faith inherited a deep distaste for anything to do with death or the handling of dead animals. This dislike continues to affect attitudes to the *burakumin*, ethnic Japanese who have traditionally been involved in butchery, leather-working or grave-digging. Formerly known as *eta*, "filthy ones", they have long been outcasts in Japanese society. Although attempts have been made to improve their lot, they still suffer from intense prejudice.

Manga comic-strips are immensely popular in Japan, drawing their inspiration from the numerous mythical heroes and the more fantastic elements of traditional Japanese stories. This ghostly female figure is one of many spectral figures and demons which continue to be depicted in the modern media.

Shinto's past connections with nationalism have also continued to cause controversy, most notably when Prime Minister Yasuhiro Nakasone chose to make an official visit to the Yasukuni Shrine in Tokyo in 1985. The sanctuary is believed to house the souls of Japan's war dead from all the conflicts of the past 120 years, including World War II; among them are those of seven high-ranking war criminals including the wartime dictator Hideki Tojo, who was secretly re-interred there by supporters in 1979. The shrine has also always had a special place in nationalists' affections – "See you in Yasukuni" was the *kamikaze* pilots' traditional farewell – so the visit inevitably drew protests from citizens who feared a reawakened militarist spirit.

Similar fears were aroused when the traditional *daijosai* festival was revived for Emperor Akihito's enthronement in 1990. In this ritual, which had lapsed for much of the Tokugawa period, the new emperor ceremonially welcomes the *kami* to a purpose-built hall, feasting them on consecrated rice, before enjoying symbolic union with Amaterasu. Critics saw in the rite an attempt to revive memories of the imperial claim to divinity, though this was denied by its advocates, who viewed it as a benign link with the traditional past.

The Continuity of Belief

Such altercations reflect an on-going debate about the future of Shinto and Japan's mythological heritage. Some intellectuals, regarding its associations with militarism in the Meiji period as an abberation, want to see the faith return beyond the *Kojiki* to its ancient roots in nature worship. For them, Shinto's true strength has always been the reverence for the natural world that saw spirits in rocks and trees and the presence of the divine in almost everything. For such people, its message is more important still at a time when nature is under threat from human activity and when pollution is a global problem, not merely one of ritual uncleanliness.

As often happens, artists have been among the pioneers of this trend. For the most part, they have fought shy of tackling the myths head on, largely because of their complex political associations, leaving them instead to the slickly drawn, mass-market *manga* comic-strips.

Individual writers and film-makers have preferred to take themes from Japanese history or legend. It is very much in keeping with the Japanese tradition of syncretism that one of the most telling works of the new Shinto sensibility should have come from a Christian: the internationally celebrated film director Akira Kurosawa. In his elegiac late work, *Dreams*, the world of legend constantly intrudes into the contemporary Japanese scene. A young boy runs into a forest in the rain and sees a wedding procession of splendidly clad two-legged foxes; another is granted a glimpse of the *kami* of the trees his parents have uprooted by having an ancient peach orchard destroyed; a beautiful snow demoness lures a mountaineer trapped in a blizzard towards death. In these magical cinematic visions something of the primeval sense of wonder that underlies the myths resurfaces; and with it goes a deep sense of disquiet at their uncertain future in a mechanistic and soullessly technological modern world.

137

Glossary

bakufu Rule of the shogun, literally "tent government" after the headquarters of an army in the field.

bushi professional warrior or armed retainer; name given to all the warriors who made up families with a military tradition.

bushido "Way of the Warrior"; the code of honour and social behaviour which followed the unwritten code of the "Way of the Horse and Bow" (*kyuba no michi*).

daimyo a feudal landowner or lord who maintained a great number of samurai in his service, all of whom swore him an oath of allegiance according to the rules of *bushido*.

daisho a samurai's two swords (one long, *katana*, and one short, *wakizashi*).

giri a sense of obligation to superiors.

hokora small sanctuary in the landscape created to honour *kami*.

inro a multi-compartmented container worn suspended from the *kimono*.

kami "beings of higher place", a life-energy recognized by Shinto as existing in all things, both animate and inanimate.

kamikaze the typhoon or "divine wind" which thwarted a massive Mongol invasion fleet in 1281.

kana system by which Chinese ideograms were made to serve as phonetic symbols corresponding to a syllable in Japanese.

magatama the jewelled fertility necklace worn by Amaterasu.

miko a shrine virgin within the religious practices of Shinto.

miyabi the cult of courtly refinement which praised the virtues of elegance and restraint.

mon family crest worn on *montsuki*.

nembutsu prayer formula used to praise the Amida Buddha and particularly associated with the Pure Land school.

ninja a group of men and women specially trained for espionage and assassination; generally drawn from the lower classes and used by the *daimyo* to eliminate rivals and penetrate enemy fortresses.

ronin name given to all *bushi* and samurai who did not serve a particular master. A number became martial arts teachers or some other job which was compatible with their samurai status (e.g., bodyguards).

samurai a class of *bushi*. The original samurai were there to protect their lord. Later the name was given to all *bushi* of a certain rank in the service of warrior families.

seppuku ritual act of honourable self-sacrifice or suicide by samurai, often referred to in the West as *hara-kiri* (to cut the abdomen), a more vulgar term.

Shinto "The Way of the Gods", Japan's indigenous religion, closely associated with the imperial family.

shirukume a rope made from rice straw which is used as a marker of the presence of *kami*, also called a *shimenawa*.

shogun title meaning "imperial general" given by the emperor to the *daimyo* who showed himself to be the richest and the most powerful of all the lords.

tenno title given to the reigning member of the imperial family during the seventh century, meaning "Heavenly Sovereign".

torii the sacred gateway to a Shinto shrine comprising two slanting upright supports and two cross-pieces, painted vermilion and normally made from wood.

uji an extended elite family or clan which exercised local control of government, religion and warfare.

wabi an aesthetic of cultivated poverty in which the imperfect and incomplete is prized more highly than the perfect and refined. It was reflected artistically in poetry, architecture and gardening.

Index

Page numbers in *italic* denote captions. Where there is a textual reference to the topic on the same page as a caption, italics have not been used.

Further Reading

Aston, W.G. (trans.) *Nihongi: Chronicles of Japan from the Earliest Times to AD697*. Charles E. Tuttle: Tokyo, 1978
Blacker, C. *The Catalpa Bow*. Allen and Unwin: London, 1975
Bowring, R. and Kornicki, P. (eds.) *The Cambridge Encyclopedia of Japan*, Cambridge University Press: Cambridge, 1993
Chamberlain, B.H. (trans.) *Kojiki: Records of Ancient Matters*, Kelly & Co.: Yokohama, 1883
Colcutt, M., Jansen, M. and Kumakura, I. (eds.) *Cultural Atlas of Japan*, Phaidon Press: Oxford, 1988
Davis, F.H. *Myths and Legends of Japan*, Harrap: London, 1913
Earhart, H.B. *Japanese Religion*. Wadsworth Publishing: Belmont, California, 1983
Guth, C. *Japanese Art of the Edo Period*, The Everyman Art Library: London, 1996
Hall, J.W. *Japan from Prehistory to Modern Times*. Delacorte Press: New York, 1970
Hardacre, H. *Shinto and the State*, 1880-1980. Princeton University Press: Princeton, New Jersey, 1989
Littleton, C. Scott. "The Organization and Management of a Tokyo Shinto Shrine Festival" *in Ethnology* 25:195-202, 1986
Littleton, C. Scott. "Yamato-takeru: An 'Arthurian' Hero in Japanese Tradition" in *Asian Folklore Studies* 54:259-274, 1995
Mayer, F.H. *The Yanagita Guide to the Japanese Folktale*, Indiana University Press, 1986
Nelson, J.K. *A Year in the Life of a Shinto Shrine*. University of Washington Press: Seattle, 1996
Ono, S. *Shinto: The Kami Way*. Charles E. Tuttle: Tokyo, 1962
Philippi, D.L. (trans.) *Kojiki*, University of Hawaii Press: Honolulu, 1968
Piggott, J. *Japanese Mythology*, Peter Bedrick Books: New York, 1991
Reader, Ian. 1991. *Religion in Contemporary Japan*. Honolulu: University of Hawaii Press.
Sadler, A.W. "Carrying the Mikoshi: Further Notes on the Shrine Festival in Modern Tokyo" in *Asian Folklore Studies* 31:89–114, 1976
Knappert, Jan. *Pacific Mythology*, Diamond Books: London, 1995
Tyler, R. (ed. and trans.) *Japanese Tales*, Pantheon Books: New York, 1987

Picture Credits

t = top, c = centre, b = bottom, l = left, r = right

Bridgeman Art Library, London/New York = BAL
British Museum, London = BM
Christie's Images, London = Christie's
Duncan Baird Publishers = DBP
e.t. archive, London =et

Images Colour Library, London = Images
Robert Harding Picture Library = RHPL
Victoria & Albert Museum, London = V&A
Werner Forman Archive, London = WFA

Cover V&A (E5554–1886); **Cover border** Christie's; **title page** BM (M4S 11.1.044) ; **contents page** Bonhams/BAL; **page 6** RHPL; **7** Christie's; **8** et; **10** Georg Gerster/Network; **11** Museum fur Volkerkunde, Munich/DBP; **12** Fitzwilliam Museum/BAL; **13** Royal Asiatic Society/BAL; **14** Christie's; **17** Michael Holford; **18** WFA; **18–19** Christie's; **19** Christie's; **20** BL/BAL; **21** Christie's; **22–23** International Society for Education and Information, Tokyo; **23** BM (1940.12–12.1,2); **24–25** et; **26** Christie's; **27** International Society for Education and Information, Tokyo; **28t** V&A (W125-1921); **28l** V&A (E3151-1886); **28r** BAL; **29t** P. Fusco/Magnum Photos; **29b** RHPL; **30** Nigel Blythe/RHPL; **31** BAL; **32** V&A (CT173); **33** Christie's; **34** Boston Museum of Fine Arts (11.7972); **35** RHPL; **36** V&A (A.48-1952); **39** Hutchison Picture Library; **40** Japanese Art Gallery/DBP; **42–43** Japanese Art Gallery/DBP; **44** BM 1927.10-14.8); **45** Christie's; **46** G. Hellier/RHPL; **47** V&A (A746-1910); **49** Christie's; **50c** V&A (1.9-1915); **50b** Dreawett Neate Fine Art Auctioneers/BAL; **51t** Mitchell Coster/Axiom; **51b** Thierry Cazabon/Tony Stone Images; **52** V&A (E3940-1916); **53** BM (JP 3496); **54** BM (1969.4-14.01); **56** BAL; **57** BM (JA OA +999); **61** Christie's; **62** V&A (A.924-1910); **64–65** Christie's; **66** Christie's/BAL; **67** Christie's; **68** Japanese Art Gallery/DBP; **68–69** BM (ADD 790); **70** BM (1954.4-17); **71** WFA; **73** Japanese Art Gallery/DBP; **74** BAL; **75** Christopher Rennie/RHPL; **76** Fitzwilliam Museum/BAL; **77** Christie's ; **78** Christie's; **79** BAL; **80** Blackburn Museum/BAL; **82** Christie's; **84–85** V&A (E.10535-1886); **86** BM (JA 3490); **87** Michael Holford (OR 261C); **88** V&A (E.3452-1886); **89** et; **90** BM (HG143); **92** Eve Tottini/RHPL; **93** V&A (459-1904); **94** BL/BAL; **97** The Chester Beatty Library, Dublin (CBJ 117(1)); **99** The Chester Beatty Library, Dublin (CBJ 1164(22)); **98–99b** BM (HG371); **100** BM (OA 13545); **101t** G. Hellier/RHPL; **101b** BAL; **102** V&A (E.10930-1886); **103t** Fitzwilliam Museum/BAL; **103b** AA Photo Library; **103r** Christie's; **104** Christie's; **105** Jon Burbank/Hutchison Library; **106** Sotheby's Auctioneers, New York; **107** Horniman Museum, London/et; **108** V&A (E.12308-1886); **109** Christie's; **110** Ninja Museum, Ueno, Japan/WFA; **112** V&A (E.4759-1886); **113** Nigel Blythe/RHPL; **116** V&A (E.11557-1886); **117** BAL; **120** V&A/BAL; **121** V&A (E.11507:1-1886); **122** V&A (E.12587-1886); **123** Christie's; **124** BM (F.478); **126–127** Christie's/BAL; **128** V&A (FE.107-1975); **130** BM (1930.4-24.1 et al.); **131** V&A/BAL; **132t** Bruno Barbey/Magnum Photos; **132b** Michael Jenner/RHPL; **132br** International Society for Education and Information, Tokyo, Japan; **133l** Joel Rogers/Tony Stone Images; **133r** International Society for Education and Information, Tokyo, Japan; **134** Rex Features; **135** C.McCooey/TRIP; **136** Manga Entertainment; **137** Ronald Grant Archive, London